Cardiff East

Peter Gill was born in 1939 in Cardiff and started his professional career as an actor. A director as well as a writer, he has directed over eighty productions in the UK, Europe and North America. At the Royal Court Theatre in the sixties, he was responsible for introducing D. H. Lawrence's plays to the theatre. Of *Small Change*, *The Times* said: 'This is a beautiful product of uncompromising puritan imagination.' The founding director of Riverside Studios and the Royal National Theatre Studio, Peter Gill lives in London and is an Associate Director of the Royal National Theatre.

by the same author

THE SLEEPERS DEN
OVER GARDENS OUT
SMALL CHANGE
KICK FOR TOUCH
IN THE BLUE
MEAN TEARS
CALL HER AFTER ME

adaptations
A PROVINCIAL LIFE (*after Chekhov*)
THE CHERRY ORCHARD (*by Chekhov*)
AS I LAY DYING (*after the novel by Faulkner*)

PETER GILL

Cardiff East

faber and faber
LONDON · BOSTON

First published in 1997
by Faber and Faber Limited
3 Queen Square London WC1N 3AU

Typeset by Faber and Faber Ltd
Printed in England by Mackays of Chatham plc, Chatham, Kent

Peter Gill is hereby identified as author of this
work in accordance with Section 77 of the Copyright,
Designs and Patents Act 1988

A CIP record for this book
is available from the British Library

ISBN 0–571–19138–X

2 4 6 8 10 9 7 5 3 1

For Mary

Characters

Neil
Stella
Tommy
Annie
Darkie
Anne Marie
Ryan
Michael
Shirley
Billy
Marge
Dolly
Vera
Carol
Len
Charlie
Bingo Caller

The play takes place on the east side of Cardiff.

When the play begins

Darkie, Shirley, Billy, Marge, Dolly, Vera, Carol, Len and Charlie are sitting together at the back.

Not all of them are facing front.

Michael, Stella, Neil, Tommy and Annie are placed as indicated at the beginning of the first section.

Anne Marie and Ryan enter from the sides.

After this, when characters leave the main action, they rarely leave the stage. Possibly the children do.

Cardiff East was first performed at the Cottesloe Theatre, Royal National Theatre, London, on 6 February 1997 with the following cast:

Neil Daniel Evans
Stella June Watson
Tommy Matthew Rhys
Annie Gwenllian Davies
Darkie Andrew Howard
Anne-Marie Lowri Palfrey/Stacey Nelson
Ryan Alex Parker/Richard Pudney
Michael Kenneth Cranham
Shirley Melanie Hill
Billy Mark Lewis Jones
Marge Susan Brown
Dolly Elizabeth Estensen
Vera Di Botcher
Carol Lisa Palfrey
Len Karl Johnson
Charlie Windsor Davies
Bingo caller's voice Anthony O'Donnell

Directed by Peter Gill
Designed by Alison Chitty
Lighting by Andy Phillips
Music by Terry Davies

ONE

*Michael, right. Stella, right of centre, waiting. Neil in bed,
left of centre, asleep. Annie, left, about to take a pill.
Tommy, left, crosses Annie to Neil.*

Neil Who's that?

Stella Is that you?

Tommy It's all right, it's me.
Neil What?
Tommy Sssh.

Stella No.

Neil You can't come in here.
Tommy I've got to. Sssh.

Annie Perhaps I won't take one.

Neil Get out, Tommy.
Tommy I can't.
Neil Go on.
Tommy No.

Neil Tommy. Get out.

Tommy Come on, don't be like that.

Neil is sitting up in bed.

Annie If I could sleep without anything, that would be a good thing. It would be.

Neil How did you get in?

Tommy The key was under the mat.

Neil Oh Jesus.

Tommy What?

Neil I should have brought it in with me.

Tommy Well you didn't.

Neil Oh Christ.

Tommy What?

Neil I said to leave it out for me because I thought I lost mine.

Tommy How did you get in?

Neil I had it with me, I found it in my pocket. Have you brought it in?

Tommy Yeah, yeah, it's on the table. See how good I am? They'll think you brought it in.

Tommy begins to get undressed.

Neil I hope I've still got my key. Don't get undressed.

Tommy Yeah.

Neil Where's my key? Give me my trousers.

Tommy What?

Neil Give me my jeans, go on.

Tommy, trousers round his ankles, hands Neil a pair of jeans from the floor.

Thank fuck, here it is. No it isn't, where is it?

Neil gets out of bed.

Tommy What's the matter with you?

Neil I keep losing things.

Tommy Get back in bed.

Neil No, I got to find my key.

Tommy No you haven't. Get back in bed, go on.

Neil gets back into bed.

Neil You're not stopping here, Tommy, I told you.

Tommy I've got to.

Neil I told you, you can't.

Tommy Yeah.

Neil No.

Tommy I've got to.

Neil You can't. What you undressed for?

Tommy I'm sleeping here.

Neil You're not.

Tommy Yeah, I am.

Neil You can't.

Tommy I've got to. Come on, let me in.

Neil Tommy, no.

Tommy Come on.

Neil What you doing here anyway? Why didn't you go home?

Tommy I owes my mother money. My father put the bolt on the door. Come on, Neil, come on, eh?

Neil lets Tommy into bed.

You're good to me, you are.

Neil Am I?

Tommy Don't be like that. I'm sorry, Neil.

Neil All right then, shift over.

Tommy Don't you want me here?

Neil No.
I wonder where my key is?

Tommy No, don't worry, you'll find it.

Neil I hope I haven't lost it.

Tommy Don't worry, you'll find it in the morning.

Neil Come on then, and keep your hands to yourself.

Tommy I might.

Darkie comes from the back to Stella.

Darkie You still up?
Mam.
You're up late.
Mam.
What's the matter, eh?
Mam?

Annie It would please him if I didn't take one. He's a nice

4

boy. He says I'll feel better if I come off them. I've been taking them twenty, twenty-five years. Oh well, he's a nice boy.

Neil Move over.

Tommy What?

Neil Go on, move over.

Darkie What's the matter?

Stella You know.

Darkie What?

Stella What time is this then?

Annie I should say my prayers, that's what I should do.

Stella What time is this then?

Darkie I don't know what time it is.

Stella Oh, that's nice.

Darkie Don't let's have an argument. You weren't waiting up for me. If I was in, you'd be up, don't blame me, all right?

Stella I was waiting up for you.

Darkie What was you waiting up for me for?

Stella I don't know, I'm stupid, that's why. I was afraid you was stopping out and I didn't know.

Darkie Mam, when did I last stop out? What if I was stopping out? If I was stopping out, I would have told you. I'm going to bed out of this.

Stella I can't trust you no more.

Darkie You can.

Stella I can't.

Darkie What?

Stella I can't.

Darkie Why?

Stella And I don't like where you hang about.

Darkie What?

Stella You goes to some places, I know you. You don't have any money. You earns good money, what are you spending it on?

Darkie Did you get your wages? Did I pay the TV?

Stella Yes.

Darkie You can't wait up for me like this, I can't have it.

Stella You don't know what it's like. I can't go to sleep if you're not in. I was expecting you earlier.

Darkie Did I say I'd be in early? Did I say what time I'd be in?

Stella No.

Darkie I can't go on with this, I thought we'd stopped all this. What's started this up again?

Stella I don't know. It's silly.

Darkie If I was in, you'd have gone to bed by now.

Stella I might have, I suppose.

Darkie You would have.

Stella I might have.

Darkie Why don't you go to bed now?

Stella What you shoving me off to bed for? I can't sleep.

Darkie Why don't you take something?

Stella No, I don't take that rubbish, I've had all that before.

Darkie Do you want me to get you something?

Stella No thank you.

Darkie I will.

Stella No, I don't want anything.

Darkie I'll have something.

Tommy What's the matter?

Neil You are. My mother will kill me if she finds you in here.

Tommy No she won't, she likes me, she won't mind.

Neil Won't she?

Tommy I've stayed here enough times. I must have stayed here millions of times, she won't mind.

Neil What about the morning?

Tommy What about the morning? Are you working?

Neil You know I'm not.

Tommy Will she come in here?

Neil No.

Tommy Will your father come in here?

Neil He won't come in here.

Tommy Will Denise?

Neil No.

Tommy Will Tony?

Neil No.

Tommy See.

Neil How can he?

Tommy What?

Neil He's married.

Tommy Well then, there we are.

Neil Oh . . .

Tommy Will Terry?

Neil He's away playing rugby. My mother might come in.

Tommy Will she mind?

Neil No.

Tommy Right then.

>   *He lights two cigarettes.*

Do you want a cigarette?

Neil No.

Tommy I'll have one. Do you want one? Do you Neil?
Do you want a cigarette?

Neil I wonder where my key is.

Tommy Don't worry.

Neil Right, I'm going to sleep.

Tommy No, don't go to sleep, I've lit you a fag.

Tommy gives Neil the cigarette.

Neil Where have you been?

Tommy Where do you think?

Neil Why didn't you stay in her house?

Tommy Nah, she does my head in.

Neil I thought you liked her.

Tommy I do. There's too much hassle. I come home.

Neil reaches for an ashtray.

Neil Where'd you go?

Tommy In town.

Neil Did you walk back?

Tommy No, I got a taxi.

Neil You haven't got no money.

Tommy I know. I didn't pay.

Neil Oh no.

Tommy I stopped in the main road.

Neil Yeah –

Tommy By Darkie Jones's house.

Neil And?

Tommy And then I said to the man, like, I had to go in to get the money.

Neil Yeah?

Tommy So I went like down the side and then down the back and over the fence and down the gully and up the side street and up here.

Neil A driver's going to be faster than you one of these days. It's not funny. You're going to get a driver who'll give you a good hiding.

Tommy You've done it.

Neil Only with you I've done it. Why didn't you go home?

Tommy I told you why I didn't go home. I can't go home.

Neil What you going to do?

Tommy I don't know. I don't know what I'm going to do. And I owes Darkie money.

Neil What for?

Tommy He got some stuff down the docks.

Neil What stuff? You're soft, you are. That's a mug's game that is. You want to quit that, you do. You don't want to do that, do you hear me, Tommy? Do you? You can't stuff your mother's wages up your nose.

Tommy I know. I'm stopping.

Stella I saw Tracy today.

Darkie Oh aye? Where did you see her?

Stella She come over here.

Darkie What's she want round here?

Stella What's the matter with you? I don't think they're very cheerful. Lisa's off work.

Darkie Oh aye.

Stella I don't think they're very happy.

Darkie I don't suppose they are.

Stella No wonder they calls you Darkie.

Darkie What's the matter? They knows what I think. I told them when he picked up with that piece, what'd happen.

Stella I don't like you talking like that; you know I don't.

Darkie Well, what's her name then? You don't even know her name.

Stella I do know her name.

Darkie They don't ever mention her name. It's all a comedy. She's my age. He thinks he's a kid. He's a rhinestone cowboy. He wants more sense, he's bloody stupid.

Stella She seemed fed up.

Darkie With him?

Stella Not with your father. No.

Darkie She'll have 'em out of there. She's not going to put up with them two much longer. She've got a baby now. I suppose they'll want to come home next.

Stella No, they're thinking of taking a flat.

Darkie Oh yeah? Where they going to find a flat? Do you know what the price of flats are?

Stella Well Lisa earns good money.

Darkie As long as he never comes back here.

Stella I don't think that's likely.

Darkie You never know.

Stella No wonder they calls you Darkie.

Darkie I'll see him. I'll have a pint with him. I saw him last week.

Stella Did you?

Darkie We had a drink. He's a kid. He dresses like a kid.

Stella Would you mind if they came back home?

Darkie As long as they behaves themselves. No, I don't mind, as long as he don't come back. You wouldn't let him back.

Stella I hope I wouldn't.

Darkie See! He's been gone two years. It's better like this, it's better.

Stella You might go.

Darkie I won't go. If he comes back I'll go. If he comes back here ever I'll be off out of it.

Stella Not likely from what I can see. He's got a new baby.

Darkie takes a pill.

What you taking that for? What's that?

Darkie I got a headache. Sure you don't want anything? A cup of anything? Do you want me to get you something?

Stella No. I'm all right.

Neil How are you going to pay your mother?

Tommy My father's going away tomorrow to work. I'll have to talk to her.

Neil What about Darkie? He'll do you.

Tommy He won't. I'll pay him. He's good, Darkie is.

Neil turns to Tommy.

Neil Why does he let you hang round with him?

Tommy And you. You know.

Neil I don't know.

Tommy You do know.

Neil Always Bobby. You're daft, you are. Put this out for me and let's go to sleep.

Tommy Don't go to sleep, talk to me.

Neil What about?

Tommy Did you go over Susan's?

Neil Yeah?

Tommy You come home.

Neil Yeah.

Tommy You stayed in.

Neil Yeah.

Stella Where have you been anyway?

Darkie You know where I been.

Stella I don't know where you been. Well, who is she?

Darkie She's just a girl.

Stella You went out with her last night.

Darkie I did.

Stella And the other night.

Darkie I did. And tomorrow night I will.

Stella You'll go now.

Darkie Oh Mam, don't. It's only a girl. I've had girl-friends.

Stella Who is she?

Darkie You know who she is.

Stella Is it serious?

Darkie No, it isn't serious. Don't. No . . . Well . . . don't.

Stella They tell me she got a baby.

Darkie I know.

Stella It's not your baby is it?

Darkie Look. No. Stop it. No it isn't.

Stella Whose is it? I doubt if she knows.

Darkie Right, that's it. I'm off out of this.

Stella You'll go now.

Darkie I won't go.

Stella Picking up crumbs like your father.

Darkie I'm not like my father.

Stella I knew something like this would happen. You should be married by now.

Darkie If I was married I'd be gone.

Stella I know. You shouldn't be home now, you should be settled by now. This is through me. You'll go.

Darkie I won't go, because I don't want to go. You've got to stop. You've got to. Every time I'm out. I'm not Bobby. Do you want me to go? I'm not my father, I'm not Bobby. Nothing's going to happen to me.

Stella You don't understand, when you know what can happen. I tell you, I know things can happen.

Darkie Yes, I know. It was an accident, Mam.

Stella He shouldn't have been over there. You've got to listen to me. Climbing. Oh dear dear dear. This is why your father went.

Darkie Why? He went because of that other piece.

Stella I couldn't cope.

Darkie You mean he couldn't cope.

Stella Well I couldn't.

Darkie He couldn't cope. You cooked him meals.

Stella I sometimes think I won't get any better, but I was very bitter, you know, upset, upset when he went after. I wouldn't like to go through that again.

Darkie You don't have to go through any of it again.

Stella I'm so silly.

Darkie You are.

Anne Marie and then Ryan enter quickly from the left, crossing Annie, Tommy, Neil, Darkie and Stella to meet Michael. Billy and Shirley come from the back. Some of the following action includes Darkie and Stella, who are unaware of it.

Anne Marie Michael. Michael. Oh dear, come on Michael.

Michael What is it, what's the matter?

Ryan Anne Marie!

Anne Marie turns to Ryan.

Anne Marie Sssh! Sssh! What is it?

Shirley I'll kill you.

Ryan Can you go in and tell them to stop?

Michael Come in.

Billy Shut it.

Anne Marie Why didn't you stay upstairs?

Ryan They're fighting, that's why. They kept quiet and then they started again.

Billy Shut it. Shut it.

Shirley Where are you, you pig?

Michael to the children.

Michael Come in. You go upstairs in the front room.

Shirley Get out, get out. Swine that you are, if you're so clever, if you're so clever . . .

Billy Aye that's enough of that – shouting like that. What's the matter with you?

Shirley You're a pig, you're a real pig, what you said.

Michael It'll be all right.

The children go to the back.

Billy Shouting like that – what's the matter with you? Loud mouth. You're hopeless, you're nothing.

Shirley Shut up you. You want setting fire to.

Michael goes to Shirley and Billy.

Billy Ay, ay you. No . . . Michael. Hey. Hey. What's this?

Shirley Get out you swine.

Michael What's this then.

Billy See, she's . . .

Shirley You don't know what you said.

Billy Sssh, sssh, no.

Shirley No.

Billy Sssh. Yes. Well. No. All right, Michael?

Michael Yes.

Billy Where's the kids?

Shirley See you – what you – They all right, Michael?

Billy They're all right, don't you worry, aren't they, Michael?

Shirley Lot you cares –

Billy All right, Michael?

Michael Aye, fair. You going to be quiet now? Oh you two.

Shirley I'll kill him. I'll kill you, swine that you are.

Billy You haven't got the nerve. You're weak, you are.

Shirley Honestly, Billy, I'll put your face in, I'll go to the police.

Billy Don't be silly.

Shirley I will.

Michael Quieten this down, eh?

Shirley Oh, Michael, please, get rid of this swine for me will you?

Michael Come on now Billy, let's quieten down.

Billy You all right, Michael? Yeah I love him, Michael, I do.

Michael You two.

Billy Where are they?

Michael They're all right.

Billy Go and get 'em in, go on.

Shirley Shut up. They're all right.

The baby starts to cry.

Oh, there's the baby. Get out, get out, get out. I'm ashamed.

Michael Why are you ashamed?

Billy All right eh Michael.

Shirley I'll kill you.

Billy Aye, aye, aye, aye. That'll be the day. You're hopeless. Get 'em in. Get the baby.

Shirley We'll leave them there, we'll leave them. They're all right, Michael?

Michael They're all right.

Billy goes for the baby.

You had a lot to drink?

Shirley I've had a drink. I've got a right to have a drink.

Michael It's firewater with you two. You get silly and then – It's not even Saturday night.

Shirley He tries to make a fool of me.

Billy carries the baby in.

Shirley You makes a fool out of me.

Billy No, don't be silly.

Shirley Don't shut me up. You do, you do. Give me the baby.

Billy Be more of a lady, ladylike.

Shirley See, he's been like this all day. He's got the needle. See, he's needling me. He's gone quiet now, see, now you're here. Now he's made me lose my temper. He's such a sneak. Get a job, get a job, get a job then, you lazy drunk swine you are. He has a dig.

Billy Aye, aye.

Shirley If he's so clever why doesn't he keep his job? He drunk his redundancy money.

Billy I haven't. You're a liar.

Shirley Am I? No job's good enough. I've got to work, why don't he?

Michael I don't know.

Shirley Because I know people he looks down on, where my dadda worked. I go up the Hayes, on the stalls, on Saturdays. He thinks that's funny.

Billy Fifteen p for your satsumas.

Shirley He thinks that's funny. He makes a fool of my friends. How do I get my veg? You're a pig, Billy, you're a real pig, you're a pig what you said.

Billy What I say? What she talking about?

Shirley Waking the baby up.

Billy She's asleep.

Shirley He's a sneak. He's gone quiet now, now you're here. You don't know, see, you bloody – he thinks he's better than me – he's been making fun of me again in front of my kids because I does a Saturday job where I used to work.

Billy I don't.

Shirley You do.

Billy I don't, I don't.

Shirley He just pushes me. He gets me in this state so I will say anything. He starts me. He makes me feel bad. See what you've done? You're happy now. You're a lazy bloody sod. I don't care, he knows I don't mind, I don't, that he can't find a job. It's not his fault. I don't mind doing this and that when he doesn't earn anything. He earned a few bob last week. He knows that don't you?

Billy Shall I get them in?

Shirley takes the baby.

Shirley No, leave them, there, they're all right, aren't they Michael?

Billy Yes, they'll be all right.

Michael You quiet now?

Shirley Yeah. He'll go to sleep now, see, now he's caused this. He's give up now.

Michael OK?

Billy What you talking about me for?

Annie I should say my prayers. Look at me. And I've got a perfectly good dressing gown. I wonder if I should go up and dressed?

Michael OK? OK?

Annie And now my leg is starting. Dear. Oh dear.

Michael OK?

Shirley I'm tired.

Michael And me.

Annie I couldn't open a bottle of beetroot this morning and then I thought of Harry. Oh dear. I used to bottle my own.

Shirley I won't sleep.

Darkie You comin' up Mam?

Stella Aye, go on.

Anne Marie Michael.

Michael It's all right they're quiet now. Time for bed. Goodnight.

Neil What time you going to work in the morning?

Tommy I'm not going. Packed it in.

Neil Why?

Tommy They put a woman in charge.

Neil So?

Tommy So what. Don't shout at me.

Neil Come on let's go to sleep.

Tommy All right.

Tommy puts his cigarette out. Neil turns on his side.

Don't turn your back.

Neil I sleep on my side. You knows I sleep on my side.

Tommy Come on.

Neil No, leave me alone you queer bent bastard.

Tommy You like it.

Neil I don't.

Tommy Afterwards you don't, in a minute you will. Give me your hand.

He takes Neil's hand and puts it under the bedclothes.

That's better.

Neil Stop it, Tommy.

Tommy Ssh, ssh, turn into me.

Neil Don't, Tommy.

Tommy Come on.

Neil Don't.

Tommy Come on, Neil.

Neil turns to Tommy.

Yeah, that's right.

Neil Do it quiet.

Annie I can't sleep.

TWO

Michael right. Neil in bed asleep. Marge carries washing to Michael.

Marge Do this for me will you love?

Michael Good morning brother.

Marge Good morning love.

Michael You're early.

Marge My machine's broken, Jimmy's away. I told him it was going, he'll do it when he gets back.

Michael I'll have a look at it.

Marge Oh no, you'll do it for good.

Michael Well you'll have to get someone in then. Give it here then.

Marge Hang on, let me check Tommy's jeans. He left £5 in them last week. It come out useless. Have you seen him?

Michael No.

Marge Wait till I see him! His father locked the door on him.

Michael Hurry up, I've got toast on.

He goes to get the toast.

Marge Is the kettle on?

Michael What?

Marge Put the kettle on.

Michael Shall I put the kettle on? Do you want a piece of toast?

Marge No, I don't really want a cup of tea. I've had about six cups. I'm all over the place this morning.

Tommy, already dressed, enters with two cups of tea, a brown envelope and five cigarettes.

Tommy Here.

Neil Did you put sugar in it?

Tommy No, I never put sugar in it, you don't like sugar.

Neil takes one of the cups.

Neil What time is it?

Tommy Late. Your mother left you this.

Neil What?

Tommy You've got to cash it for her, she left a note.

Neil Give it here.

Tommy gives him the envelope.

Tommy And she left you five fags.

He gives them to Neil.

Neil Do you want one?

Tommy I'd rather have a smoke. Got anything to smoke?

Neil These.

Tommy Haven't you? You have. Where do you keep it?

Neil I haven't got any.

Tommy Honest?

Neil I got a little bit.

Tommy Where?

Neil There.

Tommy Where?

Neil My shoe.

Tommy goes to Neil's shoe.

Tommy Here's your key.

Neil Is it?

Tommy I told you.

Neil Gis it here!

Tommy hands Neil the key.

I'll put it safe.

Tommy What else you got in here? Ah, ha.

Neil What?

Tommy Durex.

Neil Put it back.

Tommy I can use it on you.

Neil You fucking won't.

Tommy For protection.

Neil Shut up. Roll up.

Tommy Hang on, hang on.

He begins to make a joint.

Why don't you get up?

Neil In a minute.

Tommy I'm hungry. Do you want something to eat?

Neil After. Give us a smoke first.

Tommy Hang on. Why don't you get up, Neil?

Neil I will.

Tommy Here you are.

Tommy having done the honours, they smoke.

Neil What's it like out?

Tommy Great.

Neil Gis us . . . (*indicating the joint*).

Tommy Get up first.

Neil In a minute.

Tommy No, now. Then you can have this.

Neil gets out and sits on the side of the bed. They smoke.

Marge is holding out a shirt. Michael eating toast.

Marge Whose shirt is this then? Jimmy's. He says he won't wear short sleeves. When he put this on? He's got two other shirts like it he won't wear. He won't put them on. Like you, you haven't put that sweater on, you've had since Christmas.

Michael I will.

Marge What would you do without a machine? There's no launderette, where's the nearest launderette?

Michael I don't know.

Marge Up Crwys Road. For students. To think I used to get real pleasure out of washing his shirts. I didn't have a washing machine for . . . OO . . . I used Mam's. No, he's good. They're all good. They'll all put them in the machine. Tommy – all his decent clothes, he won't let me touch them. When I was washing his shirts when we were first married I could feel his mother watching me.

Michael He gone for long Jimmy?

Marge He might be back tomorrow. Even now I like to look at their shirts, if I like it, if it looks nice and it suits them. This is a nice shirt. Cotton – whose is it? It's those cheap silk ones I don't like.

Michael What's the matter with you? Talking about shirts? Don't take all the washing out. Shirts. Give them to me. What's the matter with you?

Marge Tommy, I'm checking his pockets.

Michael Our Mam used to go through all our things to see if there was lipstick on our handkerchiefs or collars.

Marge Oh, I know what I wanted to ask you. How does 'Ave Maria' go?

She sings the Bach/Gounod 'Ave Maria'.

Michael That's right.

Marge But there's another one.

Michael Yes.

Marge How does it go?

Michael I don't know. Why do you want to know?

Marge The old lady next door, over the back, her sister died. You know, she used to have the fish shop. She wants it for the funeral. She wants Mario Lanza but the crematorium don't have it. You'd think they would.

Michael Why should a crematorium have a Mario Lanza tape?

Marge I think they should.

Michael Oh, you!

Marge They don't even have 'Ave Maria'. I said I'd try and get it for her but I don't know which one to get. She wants one she heard on *Songs of Praise*.

Michael Oh, God.

Marge begins to sing.

Marge Ave . . .

Michael Shut up, Marge.

Marge Well, poor woman. *Songs of Praise*. I love *Songs of Praise*. (*singing*) 'The Rhythm of Life is a Wonderful Thing'. You miserable sod. Lovely. (*singing*) 'Morning has Broken'.

Michael No doctrine. No ideas. No morals.

Marge (*singing*) 'How Great Thou Art, How Great Thou Art'. You'd never think you were in a seminary.

Billy and Shirley come to the left of Michael and Marge.

Shirley Don't say you're sorry, all right?

Billy I'm not going to say I'm sorry. Where you been?

Shirley Where'd you think I been?

Billy I don't know.

Shirley Down the school, down the nursery. What do you think?

Billy You're lucky I'm not violent. I'm not violent you know.

Shirley Lucky.

Billy You're fortunate. You don't deserve it. You wants a good hiding I think. Only I wouldn't.

Shirley You wouldn't.

Billy Have I ever hit you, have I? You ask for it all the time you do, you do.

Shirley Shut it and go back to bed.

Billy You're used to all that, your old man used to hit hell out of your mother. This was always a rough house.

Shirley I'll get the police to you again, I will. I'll get my case taken up like those women.

Billy Don't talk stupid. Stupid. You couldn't if you tried.

Shirley I will.

Billy Shut it. Shut it you. You don't know what you're talking about. You're stupid, you look stupid. I'm going out.

Annie goes to Marge and Michael.

Michael Hello.

Annie Hello, do you want to put a bet on Michael? I'm going down the betting shop.

Michael Oh yes Annie thanks. Here it is. I want a ten p Yankee. I've written the horses out, one pound twenty including tax, OK?

Annie Yeah. What about him next door?

Michael Oh, he'll have a bet. They were at it again last night.

Annie T . . . t . . . t . . . t . . .

Michael That was a performance.

Marge Well, she's . . .

Annie I'm going round his father's.

Marge Gambling mad, you lot.

Annie I've had a bet every day since I was fourteen.

Marge Do you like washing, Annie?

Annie I don't much. I don't know what we did without a washing machine. I washed and ironed fourteen shirts on Sunday that's the first time I've ever ironed a shirt on a Sunday.

Marge Why?

Annie Teresa broke her arm and our Paddy, you know him, he likes an evening shirt. She usually does the shirts on a Sunday so I did them for her. Harry always thought I washed his shirts by hand till the day he died because I always put them on a hanger. He never knew. But then he liked corned beef from the shop, he didn't like it from a tin.

Michael From a tin? Where did he think it came from in the shop?

Annie You couldn't persuade him, he said it was different. I used to cut it thin. He never knew the difference. Like his shirts. There used to be a Chinese laundry in Bridge Street, and when I was little I used to take all the shirts there, my father's and my brothers' collars, and my brothers always said the man would kidnap me. I didn't like to go in by myself. Anyway, one day I went and there was no one else in there and the man came through the curtains from the back of the shop with his big cut-throat razor in his hand, and I ran out screaming and my brother came after him. Poor man, he'd only been shaving. I've always been frightened of Chinamen.

Michael You don't see many Chinamen round here.

Marge Annie, how does 'Ave Maria' go?

Tommy Where we going afterwards?

Neil I don't know, I only just got up.

30

Tommy I'm going to see Darkie in work.

Neil What for? You owes him money.

Tommy I know. I'm telling him I need a job. He knows a bloke, a builder, I'm going to see if there's any work, you want to come?

Neil What doing?

Tommy I don't know, plastering, anything.

Neil Plastering, you can't plaster.

Tommy I can plaster, I've tried plastering.

Neil You're not a plasterer. It'll be labouring. What else we doing?

Tommy Do you want to go swimming?

Neil Aye, all right. I haven't got any money.

Tommy I can get us in. I know a bloke on the entrance.

Neil I want to go swimming in town.

Tommy Well, we'll get in there then.

Neil How we going to get in?

Tommy We'll have to borrow off your mother, when we've cashed this.

Neil No.

Tommy How much you got? I got one pound five.

Neil I got fifty p and four fags.

Tommy We can get fags.

Neil How can we get fags? I'm not thieving.

Tommy We can get fags. Darkie'll give us fags.

Neil Why is Darkie like that?

Tommy Because he likes us.

Neil I know that. Why?

Tommy You know why.

Neil I don't see it.

Tommy I keep trying to tell you.

Neil I know you keep trying to tell me. What you trying to tell me?

Tommy Why.

Neil I know why but I don't see it.

Tommy Because of Bobby.

Neil I know. I don't get it.

Tommy Because . . .

Neil You're stupid you are. I'm getting dressed.

Tommy Because . . .

Neil Don't bother.

Vera comes from the back to Michael and Marge and Annie.

Vera Hello, Michael. (*to Marge*) I've been round your house, I thought you'd be here. I've been to get a sympathy card for Mrs Walsh.

Marge I've got to do that. You can get any kind of card in that shop but a decent Christmas card.

Vera I think they do nice cards. Do you like this?

Annie 'From the two of us to the two of you.'

Vera No – that's for my neighbour's anniversary – this one.

Michael raises his eyebrows.

Annie That's nice, that's nice – very nicely expressed. Very nice.

Vera That was a right performance in there, I heard.

Michael No, they're all right.

Vera That's always been a rough house; her father was a scrumpy drinker. You going to bingo?

Annie No. This afternoon I might. I'm putting a bet on.

Vera I heard you won ten pounds on the lottery.

Annie I did, I won ten pounds.

Marge He's all right, she's the one.

Michael Shirley – she's all right.

Annie His father was a terrible man for betting. He was my husband's best man, Charlie, they were both terrible for betting and Charlie was worse. He was a bookie's runner one time. There were three bookies in this street. He was a terrible man for betting. He had the first big payout at the Castle Bingo. He won it.

Marge How much?

Annie Oh, thousands and thousands. He gambled it all away. He's quiet now.

Vera Have you ever been over there?

Annie No, I don't like big bingo.

Vera It's like Las Vegas over there. You should see the

Ladies – gold taps and soap dishes. They went the first week, the soap dishes.

Marge What's it like over there?

Vera The toilets – the powder room I should say – you should see them. You going to bingo?

Annie This afternoon I might.

Marge She goes to them all.

Annie Do you?

Marge Yeah. The County, the Splott, the Gaiety –

Annie I've never been up there. I haven't been there since I saw – what was it? – the man who'd lost his arms in the war – Frederick March was in it. Dear. Oh well. Never mind. Well, I'm going in next door to see if he wants a bet.

Vera He still going to Gracelands, next door? He tried to sell the house to go to Gracelands.

Marge He never!

Vera He tried to sell the house to go to Gracelands. For the funeral, mind you. He wanted to sell the house. He wanted to sell the house.

Michael It's a council house.

Vera No, their other house. He had to sell it anyway. That was her mother's house. She moved back home. Still he got a pool table in there. He haven't done so bad.

Michael Yes, he's got the kitchen like a games room. They live in the front room. He knocked it through.

Vera Well, he used to have a good job. He's handy.

Annie He's all right, it's her I don't like. Rough house when her mother and father were there. He's all right though.

Marge How do 'Ave Maria' go? Vera.

Vera sings the Bach/Gounod 'Ave Maria'.

No, the other one.

Vera tries the Schubert but it resolves into the Bach/Gounod.

Vera Why?

Marge She wants it at the funeral. Mrs Walsh.

Vera Haven't the Crematorium got it?

Marge No.

Vera My niece has got it. A compilation disc. We had it for a wedding.

Michael Dear. Dear.

Marge Well, at least it's not Tina Turner, they had Tina Turner the last time I went to the Crematorium.

Annie I've never been to a Crematorium.

Vera Really?

Annie I've never been to a Crematorium, I wouldn't go to one.

Marge tries 'Ave Maria'.

Michael It's one of the conundrums of Christianity, that no one can remember 'Ave Maria'.

Neil Right – I'm getting dressed.

Tommy I'm going home first.

Neil What for?

Tommy To get my trunks. And I want to get changed.

Neil What about your mother?

Tommy She'll be over Michael's by now.

Neil Where's my trunks?

Tommy They're on the line. Where you going?

Neil To wash my face and have a piss.

Tommy We can have a shower in the baths.

Annie is talking to Billy.

Annie Do you want me to put a bet on for you?

Billy Yeah.

Annie What do you fancy?

Billy I'm having a two pound double on the favourite in the 2.30 and the 3.30 at Cheltenham.

Annie I fancy one of them. Do you want a double?

Billy Yeah.

Annie I'm going round your father's. He'll have a bet.

Shirley walks past them without speaking.

What's up with her?

Billy I don't know.

Vera I've got that money, Marge. I told you, you've got to make a fuss. My niece made me do it. She wrote the letter.

Michael What's this?

36

Vera We went on holiday to Tenerife. She booked the holiday, I took my niece, we always go. The apartment it was . . . well, you should have seen it! I wouldn't have cleaned my floors with the towels in the bathroom. A very nice boy, the tour operator. Lovely. Tim. Well, the other people were as shocked as us, and we got put in the nice hotel. We had a lovely time, it's volcanic, the one beach. Anyway, she wrote a letter of complaint for me and I got a letter back this morning, with a cheque for £50. Always complain, see. It's right.

Tommy calls off to Neil.

Tommy What you wearing Neil? Where's your new Reeboks?

Neil Why?

Tommy Wear 'em.

Neil What you wearing?

Tommy I don't know. I might borrow Phil's new shirt. He won't mind.

Neil Won't he?

Tommy We'll have a day out. Bring your gel with you.

Neil comes back in. Tommy is holding up a shirt.

Wear this.

Neil Shall I?

Tommy Yeah.

Neil takes it and puts it on. Tommy finds another shirt.

Can I wear this?

Neil No, you can't.

Tommy puts the shirt down, Neil finishes dressing.

Tommy Ready?

Neil Yeah. Towel?

Tommy We'll get a towel in my house.

He puts on Neil's baseball cap.

Neil Tommy, for fuck's sake don't wear a baseball cap.

Tommy Yeah!

Annie sings Schubert's 'Ave Maria'.

THREE

Shirley and Michael.

Shirley I haven't come for anything.

Michael What?

Shirley I haven't come for a cup of sugar or anything.

Michael laughs.

Michael Oh. Come in, Shirley.

Shirley I'm going down the baby-minder. She had the baby.

Michael Kids in school? What have you come for?

Shirley Nothing.

Michael Well then.

Shirley You're not going to move, are you?

Michael No. What makes you think that?

Shirley I'm in a panic you're going to leave.

Michael No.

Shirley If you're next door, I'm safe. You're not moving?

Michael You know I'm not moving. What do you mean, safe?

Shirley What? No, he don't.

Michael Where am I going to move to?

Shirley Just don't leave. I'm in a panic you're going to leave. I'll dissolve. I will. I'm dissolving, I'll dissolve, dissolve, I'd be gone. Oh, I'd be glad to be gone. Oh, oh. Don't go, I'm asking you.

Michael Shirley, what is it?

Shirley Say it.

Michael I'm not going anywhere. What's this? What's this? What's this?

Shirley It's just come to me this morning, what if you weren't here? You can't be certain of anything.

Michael Don't be stupid.

Shirley I am stupid, I'm dull. Dull as a stone. Dull as. Dull as. I'm stupid. Do you want me? Do you want to sleep with me? Just don't leave. I'll do anything, you know what I mean? I'm in a panic you're going to leave. I'll dissolve, I will, I'm dissolving, I'll dissolve, I'll dissolve, dissolve, I'd be gone, I'd be glad to be gone. Don't go. Say it. You've got to say it. Am I pretty? I'm plain.

Michael No, I fancy you, I – Come here. No, don't let's do this.

39

Shirley You see, you're all the same.

Michael No.

Shirley When I'm walking around here, people tell me I'm happy.

Michael Who tells you you're happy?

Shirley Oh, yes. He used to make me feel so useful, so important. As if I was someone. He was good like that; he had eight O-levels. I don't ask you to understand, just pity. I'm so desperate. I don't want to go to bed feeling so bad every night. Is me only a person who isn't anyone, only me? Only doing things. How is that free? Is you, me? Is my love for him only like our mama, our dada? My kids, who are they? I can see, but can they? Are they like me? His kids. As myself. You see. Do you think some-where – I'm not asking you to understand. You're not going? I thought, my Christ, if Michael wasn't there. He'd say make the best of it, of everything.

Michael Would he?

Shirley Use everything. Find a new use for old things, live as in a siege, teach yourself to be master of a siege situation.

Michael Would he say that?

Shirley I'm so fed up, I'm fed up. You'd think you'd grow up, you'd be your age.

Michael You're no age, you're just a girl, Shirley.

Shirley Why am I a mother, not a woman? Why are men? It makes me feel bad. Why won't someone break through, why won't someone tell me what to do?

Michael He just drinks, it's simple.

Shirley I know it's simple. Stop me. Please. Don't leave us, will you. Ever. Will you?

Marge and Vera and Dolly.

Marge I don't know who comes home to dinner now.

Vera No one I know.

Dolly My mother-in-law still cooks dinner.

Vera Does she?

Marge The kids don't.

Vera Mine never come home.

Dolly No, nor mine. Neil did sometimes.

Marge Was Tommy with Neil last night, Dolly?

Dolly No.

Marge Where was he now?

Carol wheels her baby at the back.

Vera I see that girl Darkie Jones is going out with, with her baby.

Dolly Where? Oh yeah.

Marge My father used to have a bet, have his dinner, wait for the hooter. (*nodding at Vera*) Now she has lunch in town every Wednesday with her sister.

Vera I do.

Dolly Jimmy never came home for dinner, did he?

Marge No, he always eats in work.

Vera Do you have dinner in work?

Dolly No, I'll have something later.

Vera She's a pretty girl. I've never noticed her.

Carol picks the baby up.

Dolly I saw his father's car when I got off the bus, Darkie.

Vera Len Jones, over here?

Dolly Yes, he was in the paper shop.

Marge I'd have knifed him for what he did.

Dolly New car.

Vera New car, new house, new baby.

Dolly They always spend more on the second family.

Vera Don't I know.

Marge You're well off without him, Vera.

Dolly Where'd he come from, Marge?

Marge Round the park.

Dolly Did he?

Marge He was in Michael's class.

Dolly I thought he come from town. He's Italian, isn't he?

Marge No, Dolly, his grandfather was a Somali, your grandfather was Italian.

Dolly No, he was Spanish.

Marge No, Dolly, he was Italian.

Dolly How do you know?

Marge Your mother told me.

Dolly She told me he was Spanish.

Marge He wasn't.

Dolly Well, how did she know?

Marge Well, your mother would know about her father-in-law.

Dolly We didn't know him.

Marge Dolly.

Dolly Well, why don't we have an Italian name?

Marge Why don't you have a Spanish name? They must have changed it. Your grandmother used her maiden name. I don't know where you are sometimes, Dolly.

Darkie is with the baby.

Carol OK?

Darkie Yeah, give him here.

He picks the baby up.

Marge I don't know how Stella Jones didn't knife Len Jones after that, I don't.

Vera She's only a young piece he's with, not much older than their kids.

Dolly Oh, she's years older, she's older than his kids.

Vera She's not much older.

Marge I'm glad of that. Dear oh dear, mine did all that when we were younger. All that heartache. I couldn't go through all that again. I wouldn't.

Dolly Wouldn't you?

Marge No, I wouldn't.

43

Vera I didn't.

Marge No, you didn't. Dear, dear. He's too lazy now, I'd leave him, now, anyway. I had a rough time; he's as good as gold now. He said before he went away, 'I'm not going with any dirty women, don't start.' He never went with any other women. I thought he did. He was just unreliable. He'd stay out and never let me know. You're so frightened when you're young.

Dolly I'm frightened now.

Marge Do you know, it all came back to me the other week when he went to a big funeral down the docks, and you know what they're like. I knew he'd be late, well, he said he would be, but I was still frightened. I'll be glad when we're on our own and they're all of them gone. I'll be glad when he's gone, Tommy and the other one, Philip.

Dolly Marge, how can you say that?

Marge I can. He's too much of it, staying out all hours, he never tells me, he's unreliable, he's the most unreliable, he's the most unreliable bloody kid. If I had hold of the little scarecrow, I'd put a brick through him. He's the worst of them, he is. Then on Mother's Day I get the biggest, silliest card from him of the lot. He can be a nice kid, he can also be a swine. I just can't cope with the worry of him sometimes, I wish he'd – such terrible things – now when I'm not feeling so bad about him. Not to worry again. I wish he'd go away, join the army, go to sea, they won't have him. The parents, I blame the parents. Why don't they say mother and father? What can I do about Tommy? I don't know what to do about him. They're different kids now than the other ones. He's a man now, yes, but he's been in so much trouble, and that business, you know, with Stella Jones's boy –

Vera You take too much notice of it.

44

Marge I'll cleave him when I get hold of him.

Vera You won't.

Marge I'll give him a good slap, big as he is.

Dolly I don't think you should hit your children.

Marge I don't think you can help yourself sometimes. I don't see how you could keep your hands off Tommy. He's beyond – It never did any good. You could blind him. I'd give him a slap now. But I know, if it doesn't do any good.

Vera I know. It's bad. My mother used to leather me.

Marge Well, there's a difference between a slap and a beating.

Dolly Is there? Is there?

Marge I was never cut out to be a mother. True. I'm better with other people's kids. Give me Neil. He was always like this, long before that business. Five in the morning, when he was six, the bedroom window was wide open and he'd be gone, miles away. I'd just hope he was with the milkman when he come.

Vera Oh, I like Tommy, yes he's full of life, Tommy, he cheers you up, he's a lovely old kid.

Marge You can have him.

Dolly And that Bobby was older than them, and she gets on my nerves, Stella Jones, she still blames them, she knows it was her kids' fault. He shouldn't have took them over there.

Marge She don't blame them.

Dolly Don't she. I keep away.

Marge Then it all comes back, see. I could hear them crying, right from the back of the church. I couldn't see him, Tommy, they was all down the front, the children, but I could hear him.

Dolly I didn't go.

Marge I did.

Vera Didn't you go?

Dolly She makes too much of it.

Marge Well, you can't expect people to behave better just because they've had a tragedy.

Dolly Well, you'd think –

Marge It seems as if you'd think somehow they'd be elevated and know better.

Dolly Well, we did what we could – we sent them on a holiday.

Marge (*to Vera*) That was you.

Dolly They all went on that holiday. He was a nasty kid, Bobby.

Marge No, he wasn't.

Vera No, he was just adventurous.

Dolly They shouldn't have been over there. The devil has got into her, Stella Jones, and I don't think she'll ever be happy again.

Vera Are we making a collection for Mrs-over-the-back?

Marge Yes, you take it up.

Vera Thank you.

Dolly I don't like too many flowers. There's too many flowers, it's got too much. I don't believe in it.

Vera Well, what shall we do?

Marge She's like one of those people who say they're going to give a donation, no flowers, someone else's funeral. You wouldn't do it on someone's birthday, 'I gave a donation to a good cause on your birthday.'

Dolly But I don't like too many flowers. I just don't see. I don't know why.

Marge It don't say no flowers by request in the paper.

Vera Well, I'll get a collection up then. We'll have to send a wreath, Dolly. Oh aye. Do you know someone stole my camelias and my primula, not vandals, digging them up, not kids.

Dolly Well, plants are so expensive.

Vera Next door, she's got a clever idea, she mixes lovely artificial flowers next door with her other flowers, you wouldn't know. She's a pretty girl Darkie's with – that girl. Whose baby is it – Darkie's?

Dolly It's not his.

Marge I don't think she knows.

Dolly Have she got a flat?

Marge No, she lives with her mother.

Dolly I bet she'll get a flat. They do it to get a flat, half of them.

Marge Well, she didn't. Girls don't get pregnant to get flats, Dolly, they're too stupid.

Dolly They do, you know.

Marge You listen to anyone, you do, Dolly. She hasn't got a flat, she lives with her mother.

47

Dolly No, I don't think they should get preferential treatment.

Marge They're too soft to get terminations, most of them, they're too silly. If it was that simple, it would be all right. Anyway, her mother's surrounded by SPUC posters.

Dolly Well, I'm not for abortion.

Marge Well, who's for abortion? You're daft you are, Dolly. It's funny though, these pro-life people don't seem to have many kids. Annie's a decent woman. And she won't have anything to do with it. Anything like that.

Dolly I don't think abortion's right.

Marge Dolly.

Dolly I don't.

Marge You'll upset yourself, Dolly, now.

Dolly That time, Marge, was terrible, it was terrible.

Marge Well, you wouldn't want to go back to them days, would you?

Dolly No. I wouldn't.

Marge Well, there we are.

Dolly Marge, you was good to me, that time. All times with Neil. Always. When we went to the woman, when I was pregnant. When I didn't know what to do.

Marge Don't talk like that, Dolly.

Dolly No, it don't upset me now, I'm just saying, I don't know what I'd do without you Marge.

Marge Dolly, don't now, don't. What would I do? What would I do? Who is it I come to when I have a panic, where is it I come to all hours? I come to you. All hours I

48

come to you. Who else would I run to, eh?

Vera Yes, you don't think enough of yourself, Dolly.

Dolly I wonder if she's had it inoculated? There is a scare about.

Marge Oh, a lot of them are silly.

Dolly My daughter didn't have it done. She says, why should I risk my child's life for anyone else?

Marge Honest.

Dolly Well, perhaps she's right.

Marge Dolly, you can't be trusted, you don't know anything.

Dolly What do you mean? What you laughing at? Marge?

Marge Remember when Menachem Begin died? She thought I meant the Paki in the main road.

Dolly Well, it sounded like him.

Marge Remember round the park – whatsisname –

Vera I'm sure I do.

Marge Mrs thing's son-in-law, Tina Bevan's husband – Carlos.

Vera Yes.

Marge He gave a party the night Franco died. She never knew what the party was for.

Dolly It was a good party.

Vera It's nice, that new baby, it's a lovely baby.

Marge Thank God it's not me.

Dolly Marge.

Marge Could you manage a new baby?

Dolly If I had to I would.

Marge That would be New Labour.

Vera That's a lovely shawl. I think it's handknitted, that shawl. I used to knit all my baby clothes.

Marge I never did.

Vera Oh, I did.

Dolly My mother-in-law always did mine.

Marge It's a long time since people had to knit anything. Imagine having to knit again.

Vera I don't mind knitting for a baby.

Dolly Do you always think your baby is different from other babies?

Marge You do. All my children were good babies, I was lucky. No. It's a lovely baby, I've seen it. It's beautiful.

Dolly What's she call it?

Marge Some daft name I expect. Amy Pearl, Heidi Louise. Ellie Lou. Safron.

Marge is making Dolly laugh.

Madison. Dakota. Ebbw Vale . . .

Dolly Marge.

Vera I was sitting in the hairdressers when I saw him across the street wearing his leather coat, flash bastard, holding hands with this Welsh tart. They had 'Raining in my Heart' on, which I love. I ran out and across and punched him. I made myself look common. He thought I didn't know.

Billy and Marge.

Marge What's the matter with you? You don't look too clever, Billy.

Billy I'm all right. I've been round the park. I set out with no other interest in mind than to feel a bit better. It's wonderful how simple life is when you have a hangover. Life is good. Life is good, Marge, suddenly. I can't let this get me down. I haven't had a drink. I haven't had a drink.

Marge What's the matter with you, Billy? What you carry on like that for?

Billy Oh, Marge, don't. I'm gone.

Marge No job?

Billy No, no job.

Marge Wish you were working?

Billy I wish I was. It's not that I haven't looked.

Marge Our Tommy doesn't look. He's play-acting half the time.

Billy I thought I was in line for a caretaking job. It would have done me nice. Oh, don't let's go on. It's a lovely day. Sparkling, sparkling day. Funny how it is over here on a bright day, how bright it is. Must be the reflection off the channel. And then it's so grey when it's raining. Well, I'm off.

Marge Don't go for a drink. I suppose you're going for a drink. Come and get something to eat with me. What you having for your dinner?

Billy I can't go home. I can't go home. I slammed out.

Marge Billy!

Billy I'll have to face the music. I went out this morning. Why is there love?

Marge Oh, Billy.

Billy Why do you need it? You can't tell a baby, a little baby, you love it. It wouldn't understand.

Marge You can talk to a baby.

Billy Oh, you can't only talk to a baby Marge. You can't just say, 'Why are you crying?' You know that. 'What do you want?' We've all tried that. You can't say, 'Tell me what you want, if you'll stop crying I'll get you what you want' can you? You try getting a baby down with words. Words won't do. Sex don't do it. My feelings, my feelings.

Marge Come on, pull yourself together. You're not drunk. It breaks my heart to see you like you've given up, Billy. What is it?

Billy I don't know, Marge.

Marge You keep yourself clean – Why did you marry the poor girl, the way you treat her?

Billy Why did I marry her? My father says that. He says she come from a rough house, she's a bit rough.

Marge Oh dear.

Billy That's what you think, all of you. That's what it is. That's what I think's the matter. I think you look down on her. You look down on her.

Marge Don't say I look down on her.

Billy I can't live with her, Marge.

Marge Oh aye. Hey, hey, now then.

020000 9780571191883   11.95

CARDIFF EAST

	SUB TOTAL	11.95
	TOTAL	11.95
	CASH	20.00
	CHANGE DUE	8.05

SA   117   001 12:28:01 11/29/00 3338
YOUR SALES ASSOCIATE WAS: RICHARD

Billy I'll have to find her. She's not in Shirley. I'd rather stay out. I don't want to go in. I want to stay out. I'd rather stay with you. I've been bad, Marge, I've been bad. You're great, Marge, you are. Not to be. Ha? You're a good person, Marge.

Marge Go on with you.

Billy He's away – I'll be round.

Marge You'll – like hell you will. Go on.

Billy You are.

Marge You're a silly boy. Go on now, go on, get something to eat. Don't go for a drink, don't.

Billy Not unless you lend me the money. See, I need a drink but I don't need one, I need three see and that's it. I've had it. You're a good person, Marge.

Marge Go on.

Billy He's away.

Marge Yes.

Billy I'll be round.

Marge You'll – like hell you will. Go on. I'm a married woman.

Billy I don't mind, I'm bad.

Marge You are, aren't you?

Billy I am.

Marge Are you?

Billy Yes.

Marge Are you?

Billy Very.

Marge Go home – take help.

Billy My old man give it up. He had to. He wouldn't give it up for years.

Marge I know, I know.

Billy My mother – I'm going over to see my father now – or later. Marge, you don't know the half of it. Miserable old bugger. He made her life a misery with his gambling. It's an illness and all that, like me and the booze. We should have been comfortably off. He's settled down now she's gone. It took that, and now all the others won't have anything to do with him. I go round most.

Marge Go round now.

Billy I'll go round now, Marge.

Tommy and Neil and Michael.

Michael What you doing here? Hello, Neil. Looking for work?

Neil Oh aye, yes.

Michael What, over here?

Tommy We went into town to see Darkie, we missed him. My mother been here?

Michael Yes, she's looking for you.

Tommy What she say?

Michael You'll have to ask her.

Neil Have you seen *my* mother?

Michael No. She'll be in work, won't she?

Neil Not now.

Tommy Come on then, Neil.

Michael You only just got in.

Tommy I know.

Michael Cup of tea, Neil?

Tommy Come on, Neil.

Michael You had your dinner?

Neil No.

Michael You hungry?

He goes out.

Tommy Come on, Neil.

Neil No. What's the matter with you?

Michael (*off*) What do you two want for your dinner?

Neil Anything, honest.

Tommy Hey, hold this to your ear.

He proffers Neil a cup.

Neil What? Oh.

Tommy Go on.

Neil holds the cup to his ear.

Neil What?

Tommy Go on. Can you hear the crowd?

Neil What crowd?

Tommy The crowd in the Arms Park. Can't you hear the roaring and cheering.

Neil No.

Tommy It must be half time.

Len and Stella.

Len I've come to ask you something, Stella.

Stella When they coming home?

Len Things are very difficult with Lisa.

Stella Tracy won't stay without Lisa.

Len They both don't have to go. Well, I think it would be better, it'd be better for them I think.

Stella Oh aye, I never wanted them to go.

Len Well, it seemed better for them then, didn't it? And for you.

Stella Well, they're grown women now, they ought to know what they want.

Len John won't mind?

Stella This is my house.

Len He seems well. I saw him for a drink.

Stella Yes, he said. He's very well.

Len He's got a girlfriend. That's good.

Stella Is it?

Len Well.

Stella How's the baby?

Len She's fine, she's fine, they're fine.

Darkie comes in.

Len Hello son.

Darkie What are you doing here?

Len I came to see your mother.

Stella Have you had your dinner?

Darkie Yes.

Stella Why you home so early?

Darkie Job and finish. We nearly finished yesterday.

Len On in the morning?

Darkie Yes, early. We haven't seen you over here for a bit.

Stella I told you what it would mean.

Len Would you mind?

Darkie No, why should I? As long as they behave themselves.

Stella Why would he mind? This is my house.

Darkie Yeah. Well, I'm off.

Len No, I'll go.

Darkie No. I've got to go out.

Len Perhaps I'll see you Thursday.

Stella Where you off to?

Darkie What?

Stella Where you going?

Darkie I'm going out.

Len Perhaps I'll see you Thursday then?

Darkie Yeah.

He goes.

Len Well, he seems cheerful.

Stella I'm worried about him.

Len You said he was fine.

Stella I know. I'm worried about him. He worries me.

Len Dear, dear. Oh well, I had to come over, Stella.

Stella Yes, you said.

Len I'll go, Stella.

Stella Well, I would have made you a cup of tea. Have you had lunch?

Len Oh no, I'll go home.

Stella Back to work this afternoon?

Len No, contract finished. Not till next Monday now.

Stella Lucky for some.

Len Yeah. I'll give you some money for the girls. They're both working. Perhaps you'll be a bit better off.

Stella Perhaps I will.

Charlie and Annie.

Annie Do you want anything?

Charlie No thanks, Annie.

Annie You all right?

Charlie Aye, aye, I'm all right.

Annie You owe me two pounds. I put a bet on for you. The 2.30 at Chepstow. What did you fancy?

Charlie Nothing much.

Annie See if it comes up.

Charlie The favourite. That's what I fancied. Did you put it on?

Annie Yes. I did. D'you want a cup of tea?

Charlie I owes you two pounds. No, no, I don't want a cup of tea.

Annie You're a miserable sod, Charlie, moaning to yourself and going on about old age.

Charlie Aye, aye.

Annie You want to get some exercise.

Charlie I never been fitter in my life. Anyway, I don't need exercise.

Annie What, a bloody old age pensioner like you? I saw someone helping you across the road when I was going for the bus last night.

Charlie Must have been me helping them then.

Annie Well, it was the blind leading the blind then. I saw Billy this morning.

Charlie Oh aye? I haven't seen him.

Annie You have. He was here when I was here on Monday.

Charlie Not today. She don't like it.

Annie There's been some disagreement.

Charlie She's the trouble there. How'd he get tied up with that, can you tell me that?

Annie Well, they've got children now.

Charlie No job.

Annie No job, well, you know how it is. Hard times.

Charlie I worked from when I was fourteen – thirteen – fourteen – till they laid me off. I never missed a day's work.

Annie What you taking about? You were in and out of work all your life, I remember. You worked when you had work, true, true. You and Harry.

Charlie D'you want a cup of tea, Annie?

Annie No, I've had too much tea.

Charlie Sit down, sit down.

Annie I've got things to do. Do you want me to get you a sandwich, make you something?

Charlie No, sit down, sit down.

Annie You going over to the club tonight?

Charlie Oh, I don't know. I don't think so.

Annie I'll do a couple of lines of bingo. I'll call for you. Do you want to come?

Charlie Aye, call for me.

Annie You coming on the outing?

Charlie Where?

Annie Symonds Yat.

Charlie I don't think so.

Annie I'll put your name down.

Charlie How much is it? You going?

Annie Yes.

Charlie You sure?

Annie Yes.

Charlie I might come. You going?

Annie Yes. I'd better be off. Here's your shirts.

She gives him his freshly ironed shirts.

Charlie Thanks, Annie. Very kind. It's the ironing.

Annie Now put them away. You got anything for me to take away?

Charlie No.

Annie Charlie, change that shirt. What's the matter with you? Put a clean shirt on if you're coming out with me. You got the paper?

Charlie Yes.

Annie Where's my two pounds?

Charlie I give it to you.

Annie When?

Charlie When you come in.

Annie You didn't, did you? What I do with it?

Charlie Here, I kept this for you. It's the Catholic paper. She keeps it for me next door.

Annie Thanks.

Charlie There's something in the middle interesting.

Annie Thank you.

Charlie Annie, here, here's your two pounds.

Annie You're a bloody crook, Charlie.

Charlie laughs.

Stella and Darkie.

Stella You're very quiet.

Darkie No, no.

Stella What? You are.

Darkie Am I?

Stella He's gone now.

Darkie Yeah, I see.

Stella I wish he'd come back to us.

Darkie No.

Stella I wish he would. I wish he'd get rid of them. I wish he would. It was worse than Bobby, when your father went.

Darkie No.

Stella It was. It was bad. It was worse than Bobby when your father went.

Darkie No.

Stella It was. This loss of mine. For years, you laugh and joke, at least we did, about who'd go first. I suppose you'll marry some tidy little blonde, I'd say. If you do, I'll come back and haunt you. What would he say? One of those noises he'd make, more of a snort than a reply really. He always kidded me about that, he always did. You're my boy. That's awful when I've got girls. More than Bobby. You were more wilful. That Tommy Driscoll, that Neil. Swine, little swine. I could hit him every time I see him. Useless they are, the pair of them.

Darkie No, Mam.

Stella What use are they? It was worse when your father went. At least I know where Bobby is.

Darkie No, no, no, no, Mam. No. You're mean, you are. That's what I don't like. Why are you so mean? They was terrified, Mam. They was only little kids.

Stella Aye, some kids. I know where Bobby is now.

Darkie That's what Tommy said to me. I know where Bobby is.

Stella He said it was over, your father, before that.

Darkie I don't listen.

Stella Whether or not we would have drifted apart if it hadn't been for Bobby. We might. You don't have to part, drifting apart.

Darkie Well, she'll keep him up to the mark. Look what you're doing, to make me depend on you. I'm not going to get out of this. You ask me for everything, but where are you for me? Where are you when I want you? Not here, not here, you're not here, you're not here, Mam. What did you do this to me for? You made me like this, caring for you, waiting for you.

Stella I am the devil, this is evil. Hell is a place you go to for allowing yourself to suffer. When suffering seems like sin. I try to say my prayers but I can't empty out my mind. It all seems so sinful. One time I stopped and looked what happened. No, it's up to me, I'm to blame.

Darkie You'll have to try, you will, you'll have to.

Stella How am I going to get out of it? It all goes round and round in my head. Suddenly it comes back. If I'm low, if anything happens.

Darkie What happens.

Stella Something happens.

Darkie I know, I know, and it did happen and it's not going to happen again. You should have moved away like him.

Stella Oh no I couldn't. Bobby. And now it's getting rough over here. Your father had more sense. And look what I've landed you with.

Darkie You haven't landed me with anything.

Stella You'll go.

Darkie I won't go because I don't want to go. But you've got to stop going on and on every time I'm out. I'm not Bobby. Nothing's going to happen to me.

Stella See, that's your father, that's how he carries on talking. It's awful really then isn't it – it's wrong really isn't it? I don't think it can have been sent as a trial. If it's a trial I can't overcome it. No. But it's gone. But when something goes wrong it comes back. I hear people – grief, they say – coping with it, coping with grief. Do you know what, I don't know. You just grit your teeth and hope it won't last too long this time. They thought that holiday would do the trick. Hot, in the winter. They think that makes up for things in the hot weather. It was a kind thought. What is it?

Darkie I'm tired.

Stella Are you?

Darkie I am, I'm tired.

Stella Why are men always tired?

Shirley and Billy.

Shirley I haven't been to town as it happens. You think you got me taped.

64

Billy Give me some money, Shirley.

Shirley You drink because without it you can't feel nothing.

Billy I haven't had a drink, Shirley.

Shirley You can't. You know there's more to you and then you go and have to drink to feel it. I'm tired of this I am.

Billy I'm going.

Shirley Don't go, you haven't got the money. You haven't got no money, have you?

Billy I'm going.

Shirley I'll give you money else you won't say anything. I don't want to have to pull talk out of you like a lump of sash. When you're drunk you're a bad bugger most of the time. When you're not drunk you're still out of it in another way. There's nowhere for me, you only want me when you're out of it, when you're drunk.

Billy I don't, Shirley.

Shirley And then you get nasty. Nothing goes on unless you're drunk. This is my life. You're in and out of it

Billy Oh, shut it, Shirley. I can't now.

Shirley Don't tell me to shut it.

Billy For Christ's sake shut it.

Shirley Don't you tell me to shut it.

Billy I'm not afraid of you, Shirley. You won't do anything. You're nothing, you're nothing. You wouldn't do anything if you tried. You don't understand, you're stupid, you're stupid, you're stupid.

Shirley Here, here's some. Some money. Take it. Take it and get out.

Anne Marie comes in.

Here, take her, take her and all. Go with him, go on. Go with your father. Here's money. You see, you see your cruelty. How you make me cruel, how you reduce me to the cruelty I'm capable of. Look at her. Don't dare speak, don't dare. Get out. I don't want you to go. How could you. I'm stuck with these kids. Look at her, look what you did and now it's too late to stop it.

FOUR

Marge, Michael and Dolly, right. Charlie, left.

Marge What's ethics, Michael?

Michael Oh, Marge, how do I know? You think because I spent fifteen years in a religious order I know everything.

Marge Well, you usually have an opinion on everything.

Michael Put it like this; ethics aren't for us, we just have morals. We're not material, there is no us anymore, we don't exist, we're not material.

Marge Morals.

Michael Right and wrong, sin.

Marge I know what morals are, I don't understand what ethics are.

Dolly Do you believe in sin?

Marge What?

Dolly Oh, aye, I believe in sin. It's sense. What you have to be careful is, well I believe we have a tendency to sin but you have to be careful as to what you mean by sin. I mean not everything is a sin, not half of what people think is a sin is what I call a sin and you have to be careful that it isn't like making a cup of tea with a sense of sin.

Michael And you a Catholic. You're a moral relativist, Dolly, you want to watch it. That's what we have a church for, that's what we have churches for to manage things like that, to teach us what is right and wrong. That's what Radio Four is for. They'll be after you. Moral relativism they call it.

Dolly What's that?

Michael It is the essential message of Our Lord, mercy over Justice.

Marge Love.

Michael Yes, love next to justice . . .

Marge and not pride

Dolly and not to judge

Marge and love the poor

Michael And love the poor and love the poor. I think God is everything that is good and it's our task to make God omnipotent. No, he wasn't a relativist, Our Lord. He told us to follow Him; on that He was absolute. Our Lord was a contradiction – to learn to love yourself and then to love your neighbour in the same way, that's absolute and relative. The simplest things can have the greatest consequences and if the vilest people unite, then the decent people must unite, just that. I used to remind myself that if you did good acts, something good will come of it.

Enter Annie.

67

Hello Annie, we've been talking about the state of our souls.

Dolly You should hear what he says, Annie.

Annie He says a lot of things. Pity some of them aren't his prayers.

Billy brings Charlie his winnings.

Billy I brought this for you.

Charlie Oh yes.

Billy How are you?

Charlie Not too bright.

Billy No?

Charlie What's this?

Billy Here's your winnings, Annie asked me to give them to you.

Charlie Should have put more on. Give it to us then.

Billy Hang on, let me sort it out.

He gives him the money.

I fancied that.

Charlie Yeah, I liked the look of it. Did you put a bet on?

Billy Yeah, mine never come up. One horse let me down.

Charlie Sit down, sit down, son.

Billy No. Do you want anything? Do you need anything?

Charlie No.

Billy Shall I put the kettle on?

68

Charlie No. I thought you'd be round here yesterday.

Billy No, I didn't come.

Charlie What's the matter with you?

Billy Nothing's the matter with me.

Charlie Well, it's your business. Give me a cup of tea.

Annie shows Michael and Marge a newspaper.

Annie Look at this, Charlie kept it for me. A hundred and ten years and the body is still the same as the day she died.

Dolly Who?

Annie Isn't she lovely?

Dolly Who?

Annie Look at her.

Dolly Who is it?

Annie *The Catholic Times.* Saint Bernadette. Look, isn't she lovely?

Dolly looks at the picture in the paper.

Dolly Ooh, yes.

Annie She's my favourite saint. Only thirty-five when she died. I'd love to go to Lourdes, I would, I'd love to go.

Michael I've been to Lourdes. Dear. Dear.

Annie *The Song of Bernadette* was my favourite film. I saw it in the one and nines. You had to wear a hat.

Michael Will you have a whiskey, Annie?

69

Annie Oh no.

Michael Annie, you'll have a whiskey. Marge, Dolly?

Marge No.

Annie You're not drinking. You don't drink.

Michael No, not for five years now.

Annie Five years.

Michael This is left over from Christmas. I was given a bottle Christmas twelve month. Annie likes a whiskey.

Annie Yes, I'll have a whiskey, no water mind.

Marge What are we celebrating?

Annie Nothing. My winnings – my horse came up and Charlie's.

Michael You, Marge?

Marge No.

Michael goes for the whiskey.

Annie He never drunk much.

Marge Oh, he did. Not like him next door, but he did. At one time he did.

Michael brings in the whiskey.

Michael I saw your two.

Annie Thank you.

Marge Where?

Michael They was here.

Marge You didn't say. Wait till I catch hold of him.

Michael Oh, let the boy alone, leave him alone.

Marge Always in trouble the pair of them. Taking people's cars.

Dolly They don't. Not now, Marge.

Marge No, but he'll be up to something else. No, I'm getting fed up with him.

Michael He's not so bad.

Marge Isn't he?

Michael He may not be as innocent as Kevin Maxwell or as blameless as Azil Nadir, but he is no worse than a lot of them, Marge.

Marge I don't care.

Michael You're quite right, the poor have to show better. If we don't show better then what's to be done?

Annie You going to the rugby match on Saturday, Michael?

Michael How do you think I'll get a ticket for an international match in Cardiff? It's easier to get into the Royal Enclosure at Ascot.

Annie This stadium will make a difference.

Michael Oh yes.

Dolly Are yours going?

Marge No, Jimmy will go into town with my oldest and they'll watch it in the Albert. Tommy don't show much interest in sport.

Dolly Nor Neil. I wish he did.

Marge (*pointing at Michael*) *He* was a good rugby player.

Dolly My husband's not much of a sports man.

Marge Mine is, Jimmy.

Michael Wales will never have a good side again, not without grammar schools, and they say it's a classless sport – they say rugby is a classless sport.

Marge You played rugby.

Michael I did. Your boys played soccer. I don't think worrying about the decline in standards of A-levels is going to make any difference to Tommy and Neil.

Dolly None of our kids got A-levels. I passed the eleven plus.

Marge And me.

Dolly Did Vera?

Marge No, I don't think she did. Or if she did, she didn't take her place up. You know when they talk about our children, they don't mean their children.

Billy brings Charlie a cup of tea.

Billy Here you are.

Charlie Do you want a cup of tea?

Billy No.

Charlie You need a drink.

Billy Yeah.

Charlie Get me my tablets son.

Billy Who's going to win on Saturday. Scotland?

Charlie Nah.

Billy I dunno. I don't know.

Charlie Get away man, they haven't got a dog's chance. You got the *Echo*?

Billy Aye.

Charlie Thanks.

Enter Tommy and Darkie.

Annie Hello Tommy.

Marge Hello John.

Michael Hello Darkie.

Darkie Hello.

Marge You.

Annie He's a nice boy.

Marge Is he?

Annie Well, I've never known him to be anything but a nice boy to me.

Marge Where have you been?

Tommy What do you care where I've been. You locked the door.

Marge Your father did. He told you he would.

Tommy We've been swimming.

Darkie I haven't. I been in work.

Marge Did you take one of my towels?

Tommy No. It's on the line.

Marge Did you wash it out?

Tommy No, it'll dry.

Marge I bet you took one of my big towels. You owes me four weeks money.

Tommy All right, don't show me up.

Marge I'll show you up.

Tommy I'll get your money, I'll get your money. I'll get it.

Marge Where?

Tommy I'll get it, don't worry. I went looking for work; Darkie wasn't there was you Dark?

Darkie No, I finished early.

Michael Sit down, John.

Darkie I come to see you, Michael.

Dolly Where's Neil, Tommy?

Tommy Neil! He's out there.

Darkie I told him to come last week. I told you last week that last week I told you I'd speak to the man. We finished the job yesterday.

Marge See.

Tommy See what?

Darkie I'm going, OK.

Marge OK.

Neil comes in.

Neil Hiya.

Darkie I'll come round to see you. I wanted to see you, Michael, I'll see you, Michael. OK. (*He goes.*)

Tommy Hang on, Darkie. (*He goes.*)

Dolly Neil, did you go down and get my money?

Neil Yes.

Dolly Thank you. Where is it?

Neil I left it at home on the mantelpiece, I didn't want to have it on me.

Tommy and Darkie are outside.

Tommy Have you got anything, Dark?

Darkie What?

Tommy Have you got something?

Darkie Not here.

Tommy Please, Darkie.

Darkie You owes me money, Tommy.

Tommy I'll get it, I'll get it, I'll get it, I'll get it.

Darkie I'll give you a slap if you don't.

Tommy I'll get it, my mother will give it to me.

Darkie You get it. I'll give you a slap, Tommy. I don't like it.

Tommy Come on, Dark. Please.

Darkie gives Tommy some speed.
  Carol wheels on the baby in a pram.

Tommy Thanks, mate.

Tommy goes back in to the others.

Carol What were you giving him?

Darkie Nothing.

Carol I was going round your mother's.

75

Darkie What you going round there for?

Carol To see if you was in.

Darkie Don't go round there.

Carol Why?

Darkie Don't go round there, all right? My mother wouldn't like it.

Carol What do you mean, your mother wouldn't like it?

Darkie That baby's too hot. Don't go round there. No. Don't go round there. No, don't let's talk about it. Don't go round there, all right? All right? Don't go round there.

Carol What's the matter? What's the matter with you?

Tommy has come in to his mother and the others.

Tommy Coming, Neil?

Marge Tommy, will you keep still for a little while, you're giving me a headache. Where's Darkie?

Tommy With his girl.

Marge What's she like?

Tommy She's a foxy lady.

Marge Will you shut up. What's a foxy lady? Don't take pride in ignorance.

Tommy What weighs more, a pound of nails or a pound of feathers?

Marge Shut up.

Neil Come on then.

Tommy If you drop say a car from a high building at the same time as you drop a five pence, say, which would hit the ground first?

Marge Oh, that boy.

Tommy She's great my mother, she's mad. She's a Communist. You're a Communist, Mam.

Marge Which would hit the ground first?

Michael Ow!

Dolly What is it?

Michael My knee. All the things you thought would never happen to you, you thought were the affectation of old age. Life was one long adolescence. Looking for my reading glasses and finding them down the side of my chair or on my head, and now my knee's hurting me.

Neil Are you coming, Tommy?

Dolly Michael. Have you got anything new from the library?

Michael Yes.

Dolly Anything I'd like?

Michael Have a see.

Marge You're a mystery, Dolly, you're a mystery woman.

Dolly You read.

Michael Here.

He hands Dolly a book.

Dolly Thanks. Oh yeah.

Marge Not what you read. And she draws. Have you seen her drawings? But she only draws cats and then colours them in.

Dolly I like cats.

Marge Most of her life, she thinks life is a Tammy Wynette song most of the time. You do Dolly. She can't see no harm in anyone half the time.

Dolly I can.

Marge Her husband, he can't do nothing wrong. She gets softer as she gets older.

Dolly But he don't.

Marge Well, I know that, he's my friend, I knew him before you. But they're not perfect, Dolly, mine isn't.

Dolly What's wrong with him? He's as good as gold, Marge, you don't know how lucky you are.

Marge I know, I know.

Michael Aren't you a feminist, Dolly?

Dolly Well, yes, yes, I'm a feminist. I don't have to hate my old man.

Annie I hear these women on the telly; they don't want much do they?

Michael What women?

Annie Those women with a lot of mouth chopsing on about getting their jobs, going on about things they don't know. They want everything wrapped up in the one toffee paper. Not that they're better over here. They have everything, these girls over here. Washing machines, tumble dryer, new jeans, if they want food they take it out of the freezer. They don't know what life is. Well, good luck to them. But they lives in their mother's pockets.

Marge One tiff and then back to mama. Telling their mother their married business. When I went home to my mother she said, 'I know what you're like' and sent me back. Feminism, it's for women with rich husbands or a university degree. It's too good for the working class.

Tommy Up the working class.

Marge You've got to be in work to be in the working class, Tommy. Or available for work.

Dolly They say everyone's working class now.

Marge Yes. Well, if the junior doctors find it so hard why don't they go over Panasonic for £4.80 an hour?

Dolly My niece is getting married over here. She wants to be married in this parish.

Annie That's nice, that's a nice thought. Isn't that a nice idea?

Dolly Yes, she thinks the doors of the church are nice for the photos, with big hinges.

Marge T . . . t . . . t . . .

Dolly Yes, they're going to be all dressed like the American South.

Michael Christ.

Marge Last week, did you see her over the way, her daughter? It was all Spanish. They wants their heads read. Honeymoons in Guyana, Domenica.

Annie They got it easy. My marriage wasn't celebrated.

Dolly What do you mean?

Annie My husband was a Protestant. So we had no music. No flowers.

Michael Mean, mean.

Dolly Did you have a white wedding?

79

Marge (*pointing at Dolly*) *She* did.

Annie No, we didn't have white weddings, we couldn't afford it.

Marge What did you wear, Annie?

Annie Blue. A blue dress and a picture hat. Your mother made my breakfast. You had a nice wedding. You did.

Marge I did.

Annie Yes, that's what it was like then, years ago. You know, there never used to be anybody divorced over here. Divorce, it was a rich person's thing. Well, it was more difficult for people to carry on. You knew where they were, they knew where you were.

Marge Did you have a white dress for your first communion, Annie?

Annie Oh I did, my mother made it and the veil. It was lovely.

Marge I had a dress with puff sleeves.

Dolly Mine was broderie anglaise. What did you wear, Michael?

Michael I had a grey suit and a sash. The Maltese boys all had white suits, all long trousers. What did you two wear, Neil?

Tommy Uniform.

Marge What wedding was it where the bride's mother's dressed the same colour as the bridesmaids and the grooms ties and waistcoats and the flowers? They had a horse and carriage and photos in Roath Park and they were late for the reception. Bad manners.

Tommy Damian Hibbard's wedding.

Annie That's what I mean, there's more money than sense. Half of them get divorced and half of them don't get married.

Dolly Well, I went to my niece's daughter's first communion and, do you know, there was a child and she was looking over her shoulder at her grandmother, and you know, just before the child went up to take her first communion, she pulled a switch and the dress lit up with fairy lights.

Marge Tommy and Neil had Edwardian outfits for a wedding they went to.

Tommy It was wicked, Mam.

Marge Whose wedding?

Tommy Damian Hibbard. I told you. Darkie was there.

Vera goes to Charlie and Billy.

Vera I've come collecting for a wreath.

Charlie For who?

Vera You know.

Charlie I don't know.

Vera He's terrible. You do. She's got a sister.

Charlie Oh blimey, her. She dead?

Vera Her sister's dead.

Charlie Here, blimey. (*Gives her money.*)

Billy I'll have to give you something later, Vera.

Vera Yes, I'm only starting collecting this afternoon.

Charlie Will you have a cup of tea, Vera?

Vera Thank you. I'll tell you what, it's a beautiful day.

Dolly What was all this like, Annie?

Annie What do you mean?

Dolly What was all here before there was houses here?

Annie Oh I lived in town. This was all the wilds to me. You'd have to ask Charlie. (*to Michael*) Your father would have known what was here before they built on it. Years ago . . .

Michael This was all moorland here. This was all moorland caught between two rivers, the Taff and the Rummy river. The old sea wall and the gut that run alongside it must have been built to protect animals. It was so flat and wide, all at sea level. There were all farms out here at one time, not all farms because of the tides.

Annie There was a farm here when I first moved over here. I remember running over to your mother to tell her I had a house of my own, right up there by the farm.

Michael Though whether there was much agriculture or not I don't know – any crops here – not many I should think. Too salty. Cattle and sheep. The country over the other side of the Rummy, the Lambies then right out towards the lighthouse, there was sheep farming and beyond that it was all marshes and flats drained by dykes, reens, and that was all farming. There was a lot of farming there down by the old low road where there had been smuggling there and flat like that all the way up to Newport. The old London road, the Newport road, and the Great Western railway fencing it all off. Of course, the old low road is still there out to Marshfield but now Rover Way and the other road and the new housing has

82

cut us off from the sea here and squeezed the river, cut off one of its loops. Over our old house you could see straight across the channel to Somerset and watch the shipping. There were a lot of shipping lanes out there to and from Bristol. All the cargo ships and the war ships and the slave ships must have gone past our window.

Annie I saw a ship under sail. I saw the last of the big tea clippers. Marvellous, marvellous sight.

Michael I heard some rich black singer, some rich American rock singer on about this being the land of slavery. I doubt if some farm labourer, speaking Welsh, living here on this land, had ever heard of slavery, paying his tithes. Or America. It was grand to have a bit of country. It's much better than a park could be ever. It was a mean piece of country, this piece of country. It wasn't much, it wasn't beautiful compared with the beauty of what must have been up the valleys or the vale. It's sad when you don't see a Red Admiral on a day like this, or the *Gardening Programme* encouraging people to make wild gardens.

Marge Mine's always been a wild garden.

Michael There's something shocking about all this. Should we let it all go? I don't want to live in a theme park, those theme parks up the valleys. I saw a kids' workshop given by a folksinger down Habershohn Street, teaching the kids nursery rhymes. It makes me uneasy that. I don't like it. I don't like folk masses. I thank God I never had to do Irish dancing or do bloody Morris dancing. I find all that repulsive, I do. It's all a version of the Royal Wedding.

Marge People have to celebrate their lives. You've got no soul.

Dolly Annie got the *Riverdance* video, haven't you, Annie?

Annie I have. It's lovely. I'd love to see it.

Marge (*to Michael*) You shut up now.

Dolly Can I borrow it, Annie?

Marge D'you remember when Tommy used to go over the farm, before we moved here, to help with the milking and feeding? They had a big herd of cattle and I asked him what the names of the cows were. Of course, I thought cows were still called Clover. There was about two hundred cows and it was all done by electrical identification. I was thinking of the cow with the crumpled horn in the colouring book.

Michael What was it like, Tommy?

Tommy The farm I worked on was a dairy farm, sheep and pigs as well, it was the biggest farm in St Brides. It was a lovely farm, quiet, right against the sea wall, called Walnut Tree. I used to milk three times a day, five in the morning, twelve o'clock and nine o'clock. Hard but very enjoyable. It's not there any more, it's gone, there's a golf course there now.

Annie And of course they got rid of the farm to make the old airport, in the war.

Tommy Oh, don't start on about the war.

Tommy sings 'Congratulations'.

Michael Shut up, Tommy.

Tommy Neil can do Sir Cliff. Come on, Neil. Do Sir Cliff.

Neil No. Leave me alone.

Annie You haven't been in a war, nor you, nor you. You don't remember. Do you remember?

Michael I remember things I can't have witnessed. I remember things that can't have happened. The German plane crash.

Annie It wasn't a German plane. It was a –

Michael Yes, in the next street.

Annie It was a Polish airman who took off from the old airport and he crashed, and Charlie pulled him out. He was a hero, Charlie. He saved him.

Marge Did he?

Annie The King gave him a medal. The King gave him a medal.

Michael I remember my mother put the papal flag out on VE Day, which, considering Pius the Twelfth's less than warm support for the Allied cause, was optimistic. But then my mother always could tell the difference between the office and the man. That's why I became a priest. Ow! It's my knee, it's all right, I'm all right, I'm going to live till I'm a hundred and two and then tell lies about everybody over the club. I'm the only one who hasn't had a bypass over there.

Annie Years ago.

Michael Years ago.

Annie A quarter of tea, loose tea, potatoes in the bottom of a bag, lined with newspaper, a separate bag for the veg. Years ago. Door to door callers.

Michael I think it was always scrappy over here, Dolly. This isn't much of a city, is it? What's it got?

Marge It's got enough low-life. The likes of the Duchess of York are nothing to the low life in town.

Michael It's a bit fond of itself, like Liverpool.

Annie It's like one big London.

Marge Do you feel Welsh?

Michael What?

Marge Do you?

Michael No, I feel like I'm from here.

Tommy I do, I feel Welsh, me.

Neil And me. I do.

Marge I didn't feel Welsh till I went to Yorkshire and on the way back I heard a Welsh voice in a buffet car and I started to cry. Where do you feel you come from?

Michael Over here.

Marge What about you, Annie?

Annie I'm Irish.

Michael I feel I come from here. Here. This place. This town, and then South Wales.

Annie You Welsh.

Michael I feel I come from this city, I suppose, but I also – I feel I come from just these few streets. I don't feel like a sturdy, enterprising little islander. Perhaps people like us can't feel the conscience of the nation, perhaps that's why they invented the American dream. I feel foolish and proud to be part of the tradition of these parts, of the Labour movement, of the Methodist tradition, the Welsh and the Spanish miners and the Italian cafés and the English and Welsh and the Irish. And all that meant it wasn't provincial. It was an aim to liberate Britain. The Welsh were the original Britons and it had its roots with King Arthur and Owain Glyndwr and it was more nearly successful than either of them. Nationalism is just a retreat from something that was greater. The poor bloody Welsh, they did it without killing a sodding one. They should have took up arms. No one gives a toss for them it seems to me.

Dolly Where was you born, Michael?

Michael I was born over here.

Annie I was born in town.

Dolly Over here. Where was Jimmy born? In the Bay?

Marge No, he wasn't born in the Bay, he was born in the docks.

Dolly Vera?

Marge Round St Peter's Street.

Dolly Charlie?

Marge In town.

Dolly Billy?

Marge No he was born over here. She was born down Portmanmoor Road.

Michael Where were you born, Tommy?

Tommy In hospital.

Michael All sorts born in this town. Where did the Jewish people live? Were people anti-Jewish, Annie?

Annie No, no, there wasn't much anti-Jewish feeling in South Wales, there were always too many Irish people. We never thought the Jews were like the Jews with Our Lord, Jews like the Rapports. Monty Horowitz had a stall in Frederick Street. Your mother was very fond of Monty Horowitz and then, of course, when he got rich, she called him all the names going.

87

Michael Was there a Jewish quarter?

Annie Jewish quarter? There was no Jewish quarter.

Dolly Cathedral Road?

Annie No, that was all later. Round Frederick Street. I lived in Little Frederick Street. All sorts of people lived down the docks. I don't know, Jimmy's mother would know. Louisa Street, George Street was all Spanish. There was only Spanish people in George Street. Crichton Street, Greek. Christina Street. The Maltese and the Chinese in Bute Road. There were Jewish people in Temperance Town, I think.

Michael What did the Jewish people do?

Annie I don't know, pedlars and that. There were big fights with the Irish.

Marge Low-life they must have seemed.

Annie No.

Marge Annie, what about Mary Ann Street? In town. It was supposed to be one of the worst streets in Europe. Worse than the docks or the Bay.

Annie Aye, much worse.

Marge What did you do, you lived in Little Frederick Street?

Annie My mother just made us walk past Mary Ann Street. Quick. I worked for a Jewish man in Cathedral Road. Oh, what a nice man he was. If there was a spot of rain, he'd say, Mrs Donoghue, I'm going to drive you home. The Italians, I worked for them. One family, they used to put Benjiamino Gigli up when he came here, but then they interned the father in the war and called his son up and he was killed in the Italian campaign. Dear, dear.

The following overlaps.

Carol Onde fica isso?

Vera Borrita na mu. Pita pu ina aptos o taramos?

Darkie Waxaan doonaya meel aan ku noolaado?

Stella Mae'n ddrwg 'da fi, 'alla'i ddim eich helpu chi.

Billy C'e lavoro qui per me? Per favore?

Annie Taispeáin dom ce'n áit a bhfuil an sráid seo?

Stella Iawn, 'wy'n gwbod ble ma' fe. Fe af â chi yno.

Dolly Me puede decir donde hay una iglesia católica?

Shirley Per arrivare a questa strada comu faccio?

Len Ma ha y faa shaqo hadda?

Marge Nil aon áit ag mo pháisti chun dual a chodladh.

Dolly Be' sy'n bod, 'y nghariad i?

Tommy Mi puó dire dove si trova la chiesa catolica?

Neil Mc puede decir donde esa esta calle?

Vera Ehete kamia thulia?

Dolly 'Ych chi'n siarad Cymråg?

Darkie Waa xagee meeshani?

Charlie Eu estou a procurar trabalho?

Neil Tien algun trabajo?

Stella Mae'n ddrwg 'da fi, 'alla'i ddim eich helpu chi.

Billy Psahno yia na vro japu na mino.

Carol Eu estou a procurar un lugar para morar.

Tommy Lle ma' fan hyn, 's gwelwch yn dda?

Stella Be' sy'n bod, 'y nghariad i?

Annie Tá mé ag lork áit chun cónadh ann.

Stella Pam nagŷch chi'n siarad Cymrâg? Pam nagŷch chi'n siarad Cymrâg?

Michael Why don't you speak English?

Dolly Them Somalis have got the only four bedroom house around here.

Shirley comes in.

Shirley Oh. I'm sorry.

Michael No. No. Come in, Shirley.

Marge Yes. Hello, Shirley. Come in.

Tommy Hello, Shirley.

Annie Well, I can't stop here chatting. I've got things to do. Thank you, Michael. That was a nice drop of whiskey.

Dolly I've got to go too. I've got to put the tea on. They'll be in. Are you coming with me, Marge?

Annie Tara then.

Marge Hang on then. Tommy, do you want anything? It's skittles tonight, Dolly. I'll come with you. Do you want anything?

Tommy What you got?

Dolly Tara.

Tommy Come on then. All right, Shirley. Tara then.

Shirley, Neil and Michael are left.

Michael Well, you got rid of them for me, Shirley. There's only Neil and me left.

Shirley Yes.

Tommy (*off*) Neil.

FIVE

Tommy, Neil and Darkie are playing snooker. Dolly,
Marge and Vera are playing skittles. Charlie and Annie
are playing bingo. Michael is giving the answers to a quiz
and Len is singing karaoke. A Bingo Caller is calling out
numbers. What follows will overlap.

Caller Eyes down for the first line –

Michael And the answer to the first question is –

Caller All the threes, thirty-three.

Michael Keir Hardie.

Len Thank you. Thank you.

Caller Seven and four, seventy-four.

Michael The Welsh centre in the nineteen hundred and
five match against the All Blacks was Gwyn Nicholls.

Marge You're next Dolly.

Len 'You took a fine time to leave me, Lucille.'

Caller Clickety-click, sixty-six.

Michael Dic Pederyn was hung in Cardiff Gaol.

Dolly Stick them up then, love.

Len Four hungry kids and a crop in the fields.

Caller Seven and six. Was she worth it?

Michael Shakin' Stevens.

Tommy Come on, Darkie, we're on.

Len 'You took a fine time to leave me, Lucille.' (*And he continues this song to its end.*)

Caller Nine-O, as far as we go.

Michael The Terra Nova left Cardiff in . . .

Darkie Rack 'em up.

Caller Unlucky for some, thirteen.

Marge These are nice sandwiches.

Michael Alfred Sisley was married in Cardiff.

Caller And those legs –

After this, catcalls and whistles.

Darkie I'll break.

Michael Penrhrys.

Caller Unlucky for some, thirteen.

Michael The answer is Barry Dock.

Vera I felt like saying, get your arse round here. I said, don't you ever talk to me like that, I said, how dare you?

Caller Kelly's Eye, number one.

Michael Lady Charlotte Guest.

Darkie Where's the chalk?

Caller Four and five, forty-five.

Michael Jim Driscoll won the Lonsdale Belt in –

Marge That was a bolter. Come on, pay up. You're the treasurer, Dolly.

Caller Number ten, Major's den.

Single Voice Good old John.

Other Voices Not for long.

Single Voice Tony Blair.

Other Voices Do your hair.

Michael Owain Tydwr was born in Anglesey.

Vera I broke a nail. She said was it false? I said I don't wear false nails.

Caller Doctor's orders, number nine.

Tommy Shot.

Michael Matthew Arnold.

Caller Lucky for some, number seven.

Dolly These are nice sandwiches, tuna and mayonnaise.

Michael Eleven VCs were won by the South Wales Borderers at Rorke's Drift, Natal.

Caller Forty-five, halfway there.

Tommy In off the cushion, in off the cushion.

Michael The answer is Blaenau Gwent, with a majority of thirty thousand and sixty-seven.

Tommy Yeah.

Michael Richard Crawshay.

Darkie Shut up, Tommy.

Caller One and two, one dozen.

Marge That was wide and all.

Vera Sunshine.

Caller Three and four, thirty-four.

Dolly and Marge sing 'Why Was She Born So Beautiful, Why Was She Born at All?' Vera sings 'You Are My Sunshine, My Only Sunshine'.

Caller Two and three, twenty-three.

Michael The signatory to the American Declaration of Independence, born in Llandaff, was Francis Lewis.

Caller Three and four, thirty-four.

Carol enters. Tommy speaks to her.

Tommy Hello, Carol.

Caller Five and six, fifty-six.

Michael The second Marquis of Bute.

Carol Where's Darkie?

Caller Five-O. Blind fifty.

Tommy He's playing. Darkie.

Caller Two and one, twenty-one.

Vera Her eyesight's so bad she runs after the wrong bus, and then curses the bus conductor.

Caller On its own, number nine.

Michael George Borrow.

Darkie What you looking for me for? What d'you want?

Caller Two and eight, twenty-eight.

Darkie I didn't say I'd come over.

Caller Eight and eight, eighty-eight.

Michael The Mabinogion.

Neil Come on, Darkie.

Vera You know me, I'm not a moaner.

Michael Lady Eleanor Butler.

Caller Six and five, old age pension.

Darkie Tommy, take my next shot.

Carol I thought you might come over.

Michael The first race riots.

Caller Six and nine, sixty-nine.

Darkie Why you got the baby, what's the matter with you?

Charlie House.

Annie I was holding three numbers.

Billy to Shirley.

Billy I'm sorry, I'm sorry.

Carol is singing 'Simply the Best'.

Darkie What you singing for?

Michael Tessie O'Shea.

Charlie gives Annie a drink.

Charlie Here you are.

Caller Eyes down for a full house.

Billy I'm sorry.

Caller Four and four, all the fours.

Carol I can sing if I want to.

Caller Seven-O, blind seventy.

Michael Adelina Patti.

Caller One and seven, seventeen.

Darkie staggers.

Darkie Tommy, Tommy.

Tommy What's the matter, Dark?

Caller Two and one, twenty-one.

Tommy Dark!

Darkie Get Michael.

Tommy What is it? Neil.

Michael Pontypridd.

Billy You're nothing, you're nothing.

Caller All the fours, forty-four.

Darkie I can't. Don't. I can't.

Tommy You can.

Darkie I can't.

Tommy You can, come on, you can do anything.

Billy You're rubbish, you're rubbish.

Tommy You can, come on, you can.

Darkie Tommy, Tommy. Oh. Tommy. Where's Carol? I'm all right.

Caller Two and three, twenty-three.

Michael The Welsh Regiment.

96

Marge Come on, Dolly.

Annie House.

Caller And now who'll give us a song?

As the scene disperses, Len calls out, 'Anyone want a lift?' Carol continues singing. Vera, Dolly and Marge are laughing.

SIX

Stella is sitting centre, Marge sitting to her right, Tommy's bed to her left. Annie standing to the left of the bed. Michael brings folded washing to Marge.

Michael Here we are, they're all folded except the sheets.

Marge My feet. Thank you, love.

Michael You had too much to drink?

Marge No, you know I can hold my drink.

Michael Do you want a cup of something?

Marge No.

Michael Come on.

Marge What?

Michael Fold this (*indicating the sheet*).

Marge No, give it to me I'll take it home.

Michael Come on, Marge, don't be lazy, come on.

They fold the sheet together.

Marge Isn't it lovely, the smell of washing off the line? Different from the dryer. There we are, let me sit down.

97

Let me see Jimmy's shirt.

She picks up the short-sleeved shirt.

Michael Is it long before he comes back?

Marge He might be back tomorrow.

She puts the shirt down.

Michael Oh.

Marge I'll be glad to see him, I will.

Michael He's only been gone a day.

Marge I know. But when he's away I get so lonely and then I miss our dad.

Michael Marge, don't start.

Marge Yesterday I was thinking, oh I'll tell dad that. I miss him. D'you know I love Jimmy so much, I don't think anybody could love their husbands so much, but to know you love your husband so much and then to know that the man on the white charger will never come.

Michael Marge.

Marge Scratch my back, love. I hope there's work when he gets back and I hope this job goes on. I hate it when he isn't in work because he hates it so much. He feels so bad.

Michael I suppose I've never done any proper work, I don't feel like that.

Marge Priest's work.

Michael Not that kind of work. I've done that kind of work.

Marge A bit lower down love.

Tommy and Neil cross Annie to Tommy's bed.

Tommy See, I told you.

Neil They could still hear us.

Tommy They won't if you keep quiet.

Neil What if your mother comes in?

Tommy She's round Michael's. She won't say anything if you're here.

Tommy begins to undress.

Neil Where's Philip?

Tommy He's gone down his girl's.

Neil How do you know?

Tommy Because I know.

Neil He still going out with her?

Tommy Yeah.

Neil They been going out a long time.

Tommy He's getting engaged. Get undressed then.

Neil I don't know.

Tommy Well, go home.

Neil I lost my key.

Tommy They might have left one out.

Neil They won't have.

Tommy What did you do with it?

Neil I dunno.

Tommy Wake them up.

Neil I can't.

Tommy Why?

Neil Because we spent the money.

Tommy We never spent all of it, we'll pay her back.

Neil starts to undress.

Neil She'll kill me.

Tommy When do you get your Giro?

Neil Wednesday.

Tommy Pay her then.

Neil She needs it today. I won't be able to go home.

Tommy Stay here till Wednesday.

Neil I thought your father had chucked you out?

Tommy I told you he's away working. It'll be all right if you're here. I can get round her if my father's gone. You getting into bed?

Neil All right.

They get into bed.

Now keep your hands off me.

Tommy I might.

Tommy feels for Neil under the bedclothes.

Neil Tommy, come on, stop it. I'll make a noise.

Tommy Go on then. Let me do it to you, I won't hurt you.

Neil Do it to your girlfriend.

Tommy I would if she was here.

Neil You just got to find somewhere to put it. You've got to stop this.

Tommy I know, there's a lot of things I've got to stop. Come on.

Neil Do you want me to do it to you?

Tommy No.

Neil See.

Tommy Do you want to?

Neil No, I don't want to.
Do you want me to?

Tommy Let me do it to you.

Neil Shut up, Tommy, what's the matter with you? You got a girl, or this week you got a girl. You'll have another one next week. What's the matter with you? I was supposed to go round Susan's, I'm always in trouble with you.

Tommy Oh yeah. The first time I ever thieved anything it was you started it. Don't put it all on me. Why didn't you go round there?

Neil Because I was with you.

Darkie and Carol come to the right of Michael and Marge.

Darkie I got to go.

Carol Don't go yet.

Darkie It's late, I'll have to go.

Carol Why can't you stay?

Darkie Your mother, my mother.

Carol I'm leaving my mother. Darkie, what'll I do, what'll I do? Darkie, we'll have to sort this out.

Darkie There's nothing to sort out.

Carol It's because of the baby, you don't like the baby.

Darkie You know I like the baby, he's a lovely baby. What do you mean I don't like the baby?

Carol Don't go then. Please, Darkie, please, don't.

Darkie Don't, Carole, I'm not going to do it now. What's the matter with you?

Carol Darkie.

She tries to kiss him.

Darkie What do you want? What do you want me to do? Do you want me to fuck you, I'm not going to, your mother's upstairs.

Carol That didn't stop you this afternoon.

Darkie I've had all that. I've had all that.

Carol You pig. You don't care.

Darkie I do.

Carol You pig.

Darkie You don't even know who the baby's father is.

Carol I do.

Darkie Well, why don't you say who it is?

Carol Because he doesn't matter.

Darkie No, he doesn't. I'm going.

Carol Don't go. Your mother, your mother . . .

Darkie Your mother, my mother. I'll see you tomorrow.

Carol You won't see me.

Darkie I will.

Carol You're angry with me. Are you angry with me?

Darkie I'm not angry with you. I'll see you tomorrow. I will. I will. Tara then.

Billy and Shirley come to the left of Marge and Michael.

Billy I'm sorry, I'm sorry.

Shirley Go to bed.

Billy I'm sorry.

Shirley Go to bed, Billy.

Billy I'm sorry.

Shirley Go to bed, Billy, or I'll kill you.

Billy What?

Shirley Go to bed.

Billy I'm sorry.

Shirley Go to bed.

Billy I'll sleep down here.

Shirley Don't sleep down here, don't sleep down here.

Billy I'll sleep down here.

Marge Mam said you were religious when you were a child. You can't blame Mam.

Michael I don't blame her.

Marge She didn't want you to go in the church.

Michael Yes, and then she didn't want me to leave.

Marge You always associate our Mam with pain. I don't. And you were her favourite.

Michael I was religious young, or I thought I was religious. Life is religious, that's what life is. I think all those poor people who take their lives rationally like I once tried to have lost their vocation. It wasn't hard to be religious in our house.

Marge No. Mothers and sons.

Michael You should know, Margaret.

Marge I do know. What am I going to do? I don't know what to do about him.

Michael Just let him get on with it. What can you do?

Marge But he can't tell right from wrong, Tommy. He can't. And he's so stupid about it.

Michael laughs.

Don't.

Michael Because he needs you more than you can bear.

Marge Don't, Michael.

Michael Well.

Marge I always think of her with a fire lit in the mornings and the winter evenings in this house.

Michael I don't see. There was a Papal blessing by the front door. The Sacred Heart in the front room. A Crucifix in the front room. Our Lady of Fatima in the other room. That big picture of Our Lady over the mantelpiece and upstairs there was Our Lady of Lourdes and the Black Saint, Saint Martin whatever. There were two sick room sets, one of them luminous. Dear, dear. When I

was a child, in May I used to make an altar to Our Lady
and I could never get the lilac to stand up in the little glass
I used as a vase. I won all the holy pictures in school, I
was the champion. Penny catechism, five pence. It was my
favourite joke. I never liked going to church until I went
on the altar. I don't remember my first communion with
particular pleasure. I was frightened by my first confes-
sion but then when I was an altar boy I had something to
do. The amice, the alb, the girdle, the stole, the maniple,
the chasuble, ad deum qui laetificat juventutum meum. I
served Mass every morning at eight o'clock. Boat, acolyte,
thurifer, crucifer, M.C. I was a daily communicant. Rugby,
scouts, sports, school, the youth club. It all became the
one thing. Where I could put all my feelings, all my confu-
sions about what was going on, all my contradictions.
Then there was a mission when I was about fourteen, a
mission in search of vocations, and it was run by a young
priest who made me see, feel, there was something bigger
than me and I was less frightened. He reminded me of
that boy, you know that young Irish boy I told you about,
when I worked in that Aids clinic, the one who made the
sermon about Our Lord dying of Aids. He had the same
kind of warm fervour.

Marge What was he doing here?

Michael He was on leave from his Bishop to sort himself
out. He made this modern stuff feel like the early church,
he had talent for the priesthood. They won't have him
back, they wouldn't know what to do with him. Later on
we heard that the young priest at the mission left the
church when I did and later he killed himself. Eventually I
realized I had no sense of God, that I had never had a
sense of God. I lost God eventually because I realized I
had never believed in Him. I'd let my life become nothing
but moral details. Then I realised I only understood Our
Lord as a human being, I couldn't understand anything

beyond that and I was angry. I was full of what my superiors called spiritual pride, but I couldn't find my spirit. I was all dogma and then dogma to combat dogma. I knew when I first went into the Seminary that I was going to leave eventually. All we younger men used to break the bottles of the old drunks with a hammer so that the empty bottles would be indistinguishable in the other rubbish. The women who cleaned the house for us were like our mothers. We were embarrassed seeing our mothers cleaning up for us, caring for us, doing our washing, when we'd taken what we thought were vows of poverty. Our vows seemed silly and people thought we were silly, irrelevant, not to the point, to worry about our vows. I had a vocation then, I had a vocation. If you don't have a vocation . . . It's inexplicable – vocation.

Darkie goes to Stella

Darkie I finished with her, is that all right with you? I'm not seeing her again is that OK? Is that OK?

Stella You can't do that, you can't do that now.

Darkie I can. I can do anything, I can do anything me, I can do anything.

Stella What's the matter with you?

Darkie Nothing.

Stella What's the matter with you, John?

Darkie Oh dear, I feel bad. Nothing.

Stella What's the matter with you, son?

Darkie Nothing's the matter with me.

Michael We had two houses in North America, one in Boston and one in New York, in the Bronx. It was such a shock, it's difficult to imagine how exciting America was then, just to see the shops open late. So glamorous and sordid it was. Piles of dirty snow and cracked pavements and beggars and the homeless. Just like it is here now. And the church was a shock. There were two powerful Cardinals, Cushing, who was a friend of the Kennedys in Boston, and Spellman, who was a very powerful man in New York. It was all quite different to here with Heenan. The church had real influence. It seemed optimistic, America then. There had been reform in the church and I was all for it. I didn't miss the Latin Mass, I missed the Tantum Ergo and Benediction and I missed the Douai version, but I was a fervent ecumenist and I believed that was the way forward. And that all the doubts expressed were a digression. A question of style. But of course all the time there were questions that couldn't be answered. The church seemed to have lost its claim to being the only revealed truth. And the fumbling mixed messages that Paul VI sent out to poor women over contraception made the decision for many of us. And though I was excited, I was sickened by America. We used to go to receptions given by sybaritic American Irish businessmen who were bank-rolling us and sending money to Noraid and yet these were men who were pro the Vietnam war.

Marge Perhaps they thought they were sending money to freedom fighters.

Michael Oh, Marge. It's not a matter of whether you want to die for it. But then the Buddhist Monks in Vietnam had the moral victory there. It's not a matter of whether you want to die for it, it's whether you're prepared to let other people die for it and which of those other people you let die. They were motivated by simple bigotry, anti-Communist and anti-English, without any analysis of the situation. The virtues of the Irish and the vices of the English need no more rehearsing for me. Ireland without England would be like Germany without the Jews. They were sentimental about their own tragedy. They sang songs about it. They never really thought that it could have been averted. They never put to use an analysis of these things that their church was in theory uniquely suited to. Some of them wouldn't believe that some 8 million Russians had died fighting for what turns out to have been a thousand year Reich of American consumerism. Some of the men I am talking about were in Opus Dei, Marge.

Marge What's that?

Michael It's a sort of intellectual anti-Communist freemasonry. They've just canonized the man who founded it. One of the more warming things about him was that he maintained that there weren't six million Jews killed in the Holocaust, only four million.

Marge Still, four million would be quite a lot.

Michael And the racism, Marge, their attitude towards black people. I understood why the American Irish refused to fight for Abolition in the American Civil War, that was perfectly understandable to me. Having been considered the blacks of Europe they certainly weren't going to end up at the bottom of the heap in the promised land. But one nun who I heard later became interested in liberation theology once said to me, 'Ah, but you have to remember our blacks are descended from slaves, yours aren't.' I began to be disturbed by the nature of my relationship with my parishioners. I was interfering in individual lives, that wasn't in the interest of the family or truly of the church. Just the state – whatever – the dominant culture. Not truly the church or its people. Marge, tell me how what has been going on in Rwanda or Bosnia or in Palestine or Israel or even in Northern Ireland can be connected with what happened the sixties, or in what way is it related to the decline of family values? Our Order ran the best borstals and the most efficient agencies to enable working class girls to give up their babies to middle class families, and my job seemed to be a form of family planning. One of the greatest sins of empire is the inverse imperialism that it produces and it has become difficult for us who have been colonized in this way to remember the original sin. I began to look back home with an increasing anger. Living there made me realize that I wasn't Irish. I wasn't Irish, but that I had been brought up, made to feel Irish, that I was genuflecting to a notion of someone else's nationalism and that what I thought was a universal church was being practised as a sect. I wasn't in the church, I was in Ireland, the worst of Ireland, cruel, sentimental, stupid. Do you remember on Saint Patrick's Day that woman who used to come over from Ireland to sell shamrock, the one with the leg-iron?

Marge Yes.

Michael And how we used to sing, 'Hail glorious Saint Patrick dear Saint of our Isle, on Erin's green valley bestow a sweet smile and something something in the mansions above. On Erin's green valley look down in thy love.' Erin. Where's Erin? We were in Swinton Street. My mother had never been to Ireland.

Marge Dad did once, to a rugby match.

Michael The nearest our Mam came to Ireland was a bottle of Guinness. I began to be filled with a terrible hatred which I've hardly come to terms with. The Western world at least, or, as they now say, the Northern Hemisphere, is going to become one big America. Why were they so worried? All these languages and customs will be like flashes of colour in one big America. The shopping malls will soon make it indistinguishable as to whether one is in Bute, Montana or Ebbw Vale or Ashford or Crossmaglen. Except that I expect they will eventually ethnicize them.

Marge Well, at least we have more money than our mothers. Some of us.

Michael Oh, Marge. It's the unbearable smugness that accompanies their final acceptance that the Reformation has occurred. It's on a par with having formally forgiven the Jews. I used to understand all that. As I saw my final vows – I could see my final vows coming from a long way off. So I got ill. For years I defended the idea of the church, the certain practical things it did, the certain good it did. I defended it out of my own self-hatred. I despised my own cowardice but I hated the alternatives to the church, the salt of the earth, tut tut well done, isn't life a wonderful thing, aren't people wonderful, Christianity, but I resented the narrowness I'd experienced, not having been allowed to listen to Palestrina or having been forbidden to sing songs from the Methodist hymnbook. I didn't lose faith, I lost my faith, I couldn't pray, I never learned to pray, only to examine my conscience. To defend myself even after I had left, for years I was a Defender of the Faith, how it worked, its human organization, its ability to transform itself into the good of a country as well as the bad. Only when I stopped doing that could I even go into a Catholic church. I served Mass down here the other week. He was stuck. But I was angry with my government for paying for allowing my parents to have me educated by foreign bullies. I should have thrown my hand in with counter-culture I think. When I left I found I couldn't work. When I taught or did social work, or even when I was in South America that time, I felt I was still doing the same thing, and when I tried labouring I found it was too hard, I should have taken sides. There are sides to be taken. Thrown my hand in. Thrown in my hand. Thrown my hand with who now.

Marge We're lucky to have the time to talk about it, Michael.

Tommy and Neil.

Tommy Why can't you sleep?

Neil I don't know. You. Darkie.

Tommy Why Darkie? He's good, Darkie is.

Neil Why is he good? What was the matter with him? Why is he good to us? What good is he?

Tommy I told you because of Bobby.

Neil I don't see how because of Bobby.

Tommy I'll tell you.

Neil No, you goes on about it.

Tommy I don't.

Neil You do. You don't shut up about it. You goes on about it. You makes a big thing about it. That's all you does. You goes on, you goes on.

Tommy I don't.

Neil You do.

Tommy Ssh, what's the matter?

Neil I want to go home.

Tommy Don't go home, Neil. Ssh.

Shirley shakes Billy.

Shirley Come on, Billy. Come on, Billy.

Billy No. I'm all right. I'm all right.

Stella When they say I should like to have children they want one to say I should like to have children. You had children. I should like to have children but it's become something I use when I feel hard done by. I shouldn't have liked to have had children. I shouldn't have had children. Good thing I didn't. Best thing I ever did. What good would I be for them. I should have . . .

Takes her wedding ring off.

My wedding ring's fallen off. My ring's fallen off. Your ring's fallen off. Look, it's come off. Good, I'm losing weight.

Shirley I could kill you, Billy. Come on, Billy. I'll kill you.

Billy What?

Shirley I'll kill you.

Darkie If she dies do I die? If she dies, what then? If she dies where does that leave me? Have I been like one of those babies carried full term in hope? Given all that comfort and then if she dies I, free, find I have been dead born, born dead inside her, inside me.

Neil It wasn't our fault, we never wanted to go over there in the first place.

Tommy All right, all right.

Neil He made us go over there. He was bigger than us.

Tommy Yeah, yeah.

Neil How old was we?

Tommy All right.

Neil How old?

Tommy I was eight.

Neil Then I was eight, wasn't I? My mother knew I was scared but she thought it was because he was lost. But they kept asking us. Everyone did. We was crying.

Tommy All the policemen on the estate, all the estate in a big line walking across the Tidefields and the estate.

Neil Well, we didn't go.

Tommy Kids couldn't go but you could see them from the window.

Neil I was scared all the time.

Tommy And me, I couldn't tell.

Neil Nor me, I couldn't tell, I was scared all the time.

Tommy Well, that's it, it was because Darkie knew and he asked us afterwards after they'd been searching for days.

Neil And we could tell Darkie.

Tommy I know we told Darkie. That's how they found him.

Neil But I don't see what you mean.

Tommy It was because we told Darkie, because we told him. I'm telling you, I know, because we told him where Bobby was.

Neil I don't see it.

Neil turns away and begins to cry.

113

Tommy Ssh. Don't worry, come on then. Don't turn away, don't turn away.

Tommy turns Neil towards him.

Neil They think we killed him.

Tommy They don't.

Neil We never did nothing. We told him not to go up there.

Tommy What's the matter with you? Don't, Neil.

Neil Tommy.

Tommy Let me, Neil.

Neil Tommy.

Tommy Let me.

Neil Tommy.

They are struggling.

Michael Goodnight, love.

Marge Goodnight, my darling.

Billy has brought in the knife drawer from the kitchen.

Billy Here we are.

Shirley Don't, Billy.

Billy Here we are.

Shirley Don't, Billy.

She knocks it to the floor.

Billy Go on, pick it up, pick it up. Go on. I'll pick it up. Where's the knife?

Shirley Leave it, leave it Billy.

Billy I'll pick it up for you. You haven't got the guts. Here you are. (*He offers her the knife.*)

Shirley Don't.

Billy Here. Here.

   Shirley knifes Billy.

Neil Tommy.

Tommy Let me.

Neil Tommy, Tommy.

   Neil grabs hold of Tommy's head and kisses him.

Tommy Yeah.

   Billy falls to the floor.

Yeah.

Shirley Come on, Billy, don't be stupid.

Tommy Yeah.

Shirley Billy!